Deeper Than the Scars

A Journey From Cleft Lip and
Palate and Self-Rejection to
Re-Established Identity
Through Christ

Stacey Verhoff

WESTBOW
P R E S S®
A DIVISION OF THOMAS NELSON
& ZONDERVAN

This book is a work of non-fiction. Unless otherwise noted, the author and the publisher make no explicit guarantees as to the accuracy of the information contained in this book and in some cases, names of people and places have been altered to protect their privacy.

WestBow Press books may be ordered through booksellers or by contacting:

WestBow Press
A Division of Thomas Nelson & Zondervan
1663 Liberty Drive
Bloomington, IN 47403
www.westbowpress.com
1 (866) 928-1240

Scripture quotations taken from The Holy Bible, New International Version® NIV® Copyright © 1973 1978 1984 2011 by Biblica, Inc. TM. Used by permission. All rights reserved worldwide.

Scripture taken from the New King James Version®. Copyright © 1982 by Thomas Nelson. Used by permission. All rights reserved.

Unless otherwise indicated, all Scripture quotations are taken from the *Holy Bible*, New Living Translation, copyright 1996, 2004, 2007 by Tyndale House Foundation. Used by permission of Tyndale House Publishers, Inc., Carol Stream, Illinois 60188. All rights reserved.

ISBN: 978-1-9736-9032-0 (sc)
ISBN: 978-1-9736-9033-7 (hc)
ISBN: 978-1-9736-9031-3 (e)

Library of Congress Control Number: 2020907280

Print information available on the last page.

WestBow Press rev. date: 05/21/2020

For Jesus,
My Savior and Friend.
My *hope* in you carries me through this world.
It's all about *you*.

Come and listen, all you who fear God, and
I will tell you what he did for me.
Psalm 66:16

CONTENTS

INTRODUCTION

It's the most joyful moment of a woman's life—the moment she holds her child in her arms for the very first time. Those who have come before us, though, prefer not to mention that it can quickly become one of the most heart-wrenching too. But I'm going to mention it, because that's what my mom went through. When she held her firstborn son for the first time...I can't imagine the thoughts and emotions she experienced. Between his nose and lip where bone and skin should have been, instead a canyon gaped wide open, all the way back through the entire roof of his mouth.

It was in 1979, before advanced ultrasound. My parents were shocked. Being a new parent of a healthy baby is hard enough—with an experiential crash course on feeding, changing, burping, and pacifying the baby long enough to nab a few spare minutes of sleep. But on top of the rigors of "regular" parenting hardships, my parents received their own crash course from doctors on bilateral cleft lip and palate. Quickly, they learned that some of the basic functions would be harder for their son Keith, my older brother. The cleft would make nursing nearly impossible. Without lip and palate closure, sucking through a bottle was also extremely difficult. To make feeding easier, my dad sliced the nipple on the bottle to allow the milk to flow with ease. And even then, some of the milk would inadvertently go into his nasal cavity through the opening in the roof of his mouth. It would be a battle to keep him fed. And on top of it all, they were told to be on guard for ear infections. The doctors must have noticed the looks of despair on my parents' faces as they told them about their new reality.

Doctors assured my parents that, although less than one percent of babies in the US are born this way,[1] there was hope. The treatment process, which stretches over several years with multiple surgeries, usually results in the child having a typical lifestyle without any permanent health concerns. Oh, the surgeries cannot erase all the effects. The nose is usually a little flatter. The lips a little jagged. And the scars between the two will always remain.

My parents were left to wonder what the cause of the cleft was. And although there are some factors that increase the risk, it was impossible to know the cause for certain. My parents went on to have two more children, a girl and then another boy. Both were born healthy. I can't say they are *normal*—they are my older siblings after all. But they were given a clean bill of health.

Then I was born, six years after my oldest brother. Once again, my mom would have that familiar feeling—the happiest moment of her life mixed with the heart-wrenching feeling that something had gone very wrong. Bilateral cleft lip and palate....again. It was twice as unlikely for girls, but here they stood. I wonder how my parents must have felt in that moment—whether it was more or less frightening, knowing how my oldest brother suffered through surgeries, teasing, bullies, and self-esteem issues. And they must have wondered if it would be even harder for a girl, whose self-worth is often wrapped up in her appearance. I went through the same operations. And I was left with the similar physical scars as my brother.

Now at 33 years of age, with my last surgery completed over 10 years ago, at random times, someone still asks, "How did you get those scars on your lip?" In the past, each time someone would ask about my scars, I felt the solid ground beneath me turning to quicksand. An internal discomfort overcame me. Unprepared to give an adequate response I would mumble, "I was born this way" and carried on the conversation as if the question had never been asked.

Reflecting on these awkward moments, I began to ponder how I could better answer the question.

This is the story behind my scars. Yes, it is a story of physical reconstruction, but it goes far deeper than the scars on my lip. This story goes deeper to reveal the wounds and the healing of my heart. This healing has not happened over night but has been an ongoing process over many years. Even today, God continues to work on my inner transformation, helping me see this life from His perspective rather than my own.

Although my scars had been a source of embarrassment and insecurity, I'm learning to see my scars as a beautiful thing. Scars are beautiful because they not only tell the story of what happened to us, but they tell of what happened *within us*. They tell of what we're in the process of overcoming and what we've already overcome.

The scars on my face represent my personal journey with God. They represent Him walking me through countless surgeries, speech therapy, multiple ear infections, hearing loss, and extensive dental work. He led me. Not only over those hurdles, but also through the challenges of receiving hurtful comments about my appearance. These scars. They represent the building of my faith, reliance, and trust in Him. His kind hand leading me to find my identity and value in Him when I couldn't find it in anything this world offered.

In my deepest doubts and insecurities, *God was there.*

Each time I see my scars I remember; through it all, *He held me secure.*

CHAPTER 1

Leaving the Past in the Past

"You can't start the next chapter of your life if you keep re-reading the last one."

- Author Unknown

"If you can't fly, then run, if you can't run, then walk, if you can't walk, then crawl, but whatever you do, you have to keep moving forward."

- Martin Luther King Jr

Most of the emotional scars that I have from childhood came in the form of teasing words—for being born with a bilateral cleft lip and palate. Comments like, "You look ugly," or questions such as, "Did you get hit in the face with a shovel?" quickly left their penetrating marks on my heart. Some instances I still remember clearly to this day. Those are the ones that cut the deepest. In elementary school, I was playing basketball on the playground with a few peers. After deflecting off the fingertips of my classmate, our ball rolled out of bounds toward a group of older boys. Snatching the basketball, they refused to give it back. We requested many times. Finally, we made one last request, letting the boys know that we'd next be going to an adult for help if they wouldn't give it back. They agreed at last. Holding the ball with outstretched arms, one boy came towards me. He pushed his nose flat with his index finger, teasing, "Here's your ball flat nose."

I no longer wanted the ball.

I was too upset.

His words hit deep like arrows into my heart.

Later that same year, my classmates and I completed a school project. We created a cutout of the side profile of our faces. Using an overhead projector, the light source created a shadow of the side of my face, which projected onto the wall. As I stood incredibly still, the teacher traced the shape of my face onto colored paper. It was my job to cut along her lines. When completed, we hung our finished projects on the wall.

Although it was fun playing with the light, I didn't like seeing my shape—the curves, drop-offs, or flat cliffs—next to my classmates' more uniform faces. I learned the definition of my *side profile*. I also learned I did *not* like mine. Each time I looked at my cutout, I couldn't help but agree with the words with which others taunted me. When I looked at my nose from the side, it did appear *flat*.

The name *flat nose* taught me that my nose was flatter than the rest of the kids. These hurtful comments had me looking at my side profile in the mirror to examine the height of my nose and left me scanning around the classroom, subjectively measuring the height of the noses seated around me. Those words were now ingrained in my mind. I spent time after each surgery assessing the new status of my nose, hoping that it was worth the pain and no longer appeared flat. Although my nose did improve with many surgeries, it never reached what I had hoped.

During one of my high school basketball games, a few students would chant, "Flat nose!" each time I was within hearing distance. As I heard them, the comments fired me up and made me play much harder to ensure we beat their team. However, these words often lingered in my mind and heart long after the game was over. Already believing I was ugly, my peers' words began to confirm my feelings of inadequacy. Remember the old saying, "Sticks and stones may break my bones, but names will never hurt me?" While it's true that words don't cause physical pain, names do hurt. They often become a label we retain into adulthood.

Even in adulthood, if someone mentioned my sister and I looked alike, I thought, "Well maybe because we both have blonde hair; but she doesn't have a flat nose like me." Some girls enjoy getting a makeover. I dreaded receiving an invitation to these parties. I didn't want anyone noticing my flat nose or scars while determining which shade of blush looked best on me. No matter the context, *flat* was the only adjective I used to describe my nose.

Understanding the Source of the Hurtful Words

While it may seem a bit overly sensitive to some, it's not easy to move past the hurtful words of our childhood and refuse them permission to linger into our adult years. For me, letting go of those hurtful words has been a process of understanding the *source* of the words. Through my experience, I found that hurtful words came from three different sources: the curious kid, the remorseful kid, and the mean-spirited kid. If I could go back in time and teach my school-aged self about the different kinds of kids, here is what I would say:

The Curious Kid: Some kids are just curious. These kids ask questions to understand what happened to you. Just as they ask their parents many questions about why the sun is hot, how an airplane flies, and where bears go in the winter, they are exploring the world around them. They are learning what it means to have a birth defect. At this point in their life, they are still developing social skills. While the way they ask the question is not always socially appropriate, they really do not mean any harm or malice. Other children are simply empathetic and have compassionate hearts. With a sympathetic look, they will ask about the *ouchy* on your face and may want to share a *booboo* story of their own or just offer a compassionate hug. They may feel that by knowing about and relating to your situation, it will somehow help.

The Remorseful Kid: Next, I would tell my younger self about the remorseful kids. Some of the kids, who make intentional and hurtful comments will one day, by God's grace, reconsider and regret saying those words. As they grow and mature, as God changes their hearts and minds, a few who made fun of you in elementary school may even become your high school friends. For others, life has a way of shaping us. Some of the kids that make fun of you today may one day even have a child of their own with a birth defect. Now experiencing your pain firsthand, they may feel even more remorseful as they navigate the challenging waters with their own child.

The Mean-Spirited Kid: Finally, I would tell my younger self that some of the kids that called you names in elementary, junior high, and high school are just plain means kids. They will later become mean adults. While most grow up and mature, not all do. A few of those mean kids will be mean the rest of their lives--*not only to you,* but really to almost everyone, including their own spouses and children.

These individuals are the definition of hurting people who hurt other people. They are dealing with their own internal and external issues and are choosing to dish out their hurt on you. You are simply a target for their pain. It really is not a reflection of you at all; it's more of a reflection of the issues within *their* own hearts and minds.

These children might simply be a product of their environment and are doing what their parents have modeled. Some of them will thankfully overcome and break the cycle. But for those who don't break the cycle, in just a few short years, you can fully see the effects of a calloused and unrepentant heart. When you see the misery in which mean people live, knowing that it does not have to be this way, your heart will hurt for them. When you see the destructive paths that their lives take, your heart will break more for their broken lives than the names they called you in grade school.

My Training Ground

After my basketball-playing days were over, I decided to join the dark side and become a basketball referee. During my playing days, I was guilty of thinking referees were all against me and in desperate need of prescription glasses. While joining the ranks, I found that being a referee is actually an incredibly difficult job. It requires having tough skin, as some fans can say some nasty comments.

There are two basic job requirements to be a basketball official: 1. You have to be insane enough to subject yourself to verbal abuse, and 2. You also have to be crazy enough to wear a uniform that sends the fashion police on hot pursuit. My uniform includes a striped shirt, black-pleated pants, and shiny black New Balance shoes that make any man over the age of seventy jealous. Already suffering from a conductive hearing loss due to frequent ear infections, I wear noise-canceling earplugs to prevent further damage from the loud and high-pitched whistle. The filter allows me to hear what I need to hear—coaches calling for timeouts or asking questions, without hearing the screeching whistle.

While most fans are decent people and good sports, a few fans are plain mean. One night, I came across a man who took his self-nominated job of being a supportive fan to a completely new level. From the top row of the bleachers, I could hear this man screaming at me each time I made a call. It didn't matter what call I made. He yelled. While most fans complain and then give it a rest, this man wouldn't stop. All game long.

He. Would. Not. Stop.

This man was *so* loud. Even with my noise-canceling earplugs in, I could still hear him! Although I heard him yelling, the earplugs deadened the sound. I could only make out a few words. Muffled, it sounded like Charlie Brown, "Wah, wah, wah, you wah, wah, *horrible.*"

If I took my attention off the game and really focused on what he was yelling, I could understand more. But why would I want to do that? The teams were playing a game right in front of me, and that was the reason I was there. That night, I appreciated my noise-cancelling earplugs. His yelling became meaningless background noise. Without giving his comments a front row in my head, I was free to focus on the game in front of me and do my very best job officiating.

At times in our lives, we're all going to experience the angry man in the stands. He is going to yell. He is angry at life and wants to yell about everything. It had nothing to do with me; *he didn't even know me.* I was just a target for his anger. After the game was over, I would be officiating a different game. He would be in the same seat each game, just yelling at different officials, telling them the same message he told me. To him, *everything is horrible.*

Just as I'm free to ignore the angry man in the stands, I'm free to ignore the *flat nose* comments of my past. In the moments when the hurtful words fly, I have a choice to put on my noise-canceling earplugs and *live my own life well.* From individuals like him, these destructive words really do not deserve my attention and focus.

Looking back at the hurtful names, I learned the real question was not, "Why are you so ugly; did you get hit in the face with a shovel?" The real question to ask was, "Why are those mean kids so angry?" What makes them hurt so much that they feel the need to try to hurt me? What is tearing them up on the inside that they feel the need to lash out against others? Has anyone ever told them that God loves them and they, too, are fearfully and wonderfully made?

Seeking Truthful Perspective

One of the most humbling aspects of officiating is that it quickly reminds me that I'm far from perfect. Although I'm capable of making correct calls, I'm equally human and will make the wrong call at times. After making a controversial call at the end of a game in which the coach clearly did not agree, I began replaying the situation in my head. Slowing the play down, I questioned if I made the right call or if the coach had justification for being upset.

Wondering if I blew the call, I picked up the phone and called a fellow official who happened to be at the game watching his daughter. Our discussion included the rules of the game to determine why the play was illegal. Although the call was technically correct, we discussed ways I could better handle a similar situation in the future.

I am all ears to *constructive* criticism but not from the angry man in the stands. Although the angry man and fellow official both provided me feedback on my performance, I received the fellow official's comments because he knows me. He is in the trenches of officiating with me. The man in the stands has never opened the rulebook.

Everyone has an opinion but not everyone is willing to get on the court and make the tough calls of officiating. The rude and unhelpful comment came from the person sitting in the nosebleeds who has not taken a moment to get to know me. He thinks I'm just a "zebra" running around in a striped shirt. He fails to realize I'm someone's daughter, sister, and friend.

Just as the bleachers in the gym are filled with naysayers and those that try to bring us down, so are the bleachers of our lives. However, amongst those naysayers are genuine people who care for us and want to encourage our hearts. These people, who offer the truth from a perspective we cannot see for ourselves, are whom we should listen to.

During my most insecure times, I can now better appreciate others who offered a different perspective from my narrowed tunnel vision that the cleft lip and palate made me ugly. When talking to my friend Carly about how the cleft was a physical deformity, she commented that she didn't see it as a deformity. She just thinks it's *different from the majority.*

She continued to say that it may be a challenge for eating and speaking but once the corrective surgeries are complete, those affects are no longer present. I told her I appreciated her perspective, but I had to admit I wasn't in full agreement. Even after the completion of my corrective surgeries, at times, I still felt I looked deformed. It was a little difficult for me not to label my cleft as a deformity, as I had seen it that way my entire life. Her response was incredibly profound; one I will never forget. She replied:

"Of course it would be a challenge for you to accept; you're on the basketball court, and I'm in the bleachers."

Her analogy of the bleachers brought me back to a special time in my life, my high school basketball days. During my high school basketball games, my dad sat in the bleachers and with a simple gesture or the mouthing of words, he would give me encouragement when I looked his way. Just as my dad was in the bleachers at my basketball games, he and others were sitting in the bleachers of my life, offering me encouragement along the way.

My friend, who was offering encouragement to my heart, knew she had a different view because she hadn't walked a day in my shoes. She was sitting in her spot in the bleachers of my life, sharing her viewpoint but she had no skin in the game. I was on the basketball court, wearing the bruises and emotions of my battle and couldn't see what she could see from the bleachers. She could have told me that she was right and I was wrong. She could have mentioned all the other people who would agree with her. She didn't condemn me for my thoughts. She simply invited me to see from a different perspective.

Although I still wrestle with this perspective to this day, I do know one thing: we need good people in the bleachers of our lives, to encourage us and help us see from a different viewpoint. They help us see what we couldn't when we're in the midst of fighting our own battles. Instead of listening to the negative remarks of a few naysayers, I choose to listen to the encouraging words from the wonderful family and friends that God has placed in my life. I want to be all ears to the woman who rocked me in the wee hours of the night and the man who worked 50-60 hours a week to provide for my care. I want to be all ears to the friend who gets me, who laughs so hard with me until we cry tears.

Above all, when God, my creator, sustainer and nourisher speaks, I want to hear Him! When the hurtful words of our past rear their ugly head, we can remember God carries the *final* word on our lives. Nothing that's ever said against us is bigger than what God has already said. While others' words have the power to encourage or discourage us, God's Word is living and active and has the power to transform us to the very core.[1]

God's Word is the Gold Standard of our lives, not the opinions of others.

Learning to decipher God's truth from a lie has been a gift that continues to give to me in every season of my life. When I began to consistently study the Word of God, I stopped focusing on the names I was once called. With my mind overwhelmed by the amazing truth that God created me, called His creation "very good," and marked the human race as the crown of creation, it's difficult to continue thinking about what another kid called me in the third grade. With my mind anchored on the Word of God, no other word carries the same weight or holds the same value.

We learn that not all words are created equal.

When we hold the gold of God's Word in our mind and heart, it's hard to be distracted by the one-cent comments so freely offered by those who try to offend. By seeing that there is different value in another's comments, our emotions do not bend to every word spoken. Instead, those hurtful and untrue comments remain where they should be, far in the past and far from our mind.

Rehearsing the Past

Mentally and verbally rehearsing the hurtful moments is the easiest way to remain a prisoner to our past. With a fresh wound, it's easy to hold private conversations in our mind and hash through the multitude of zingers we wish we had slung back in the moment. In our mind's eye, we continually replay the situation, imagining ourselves putting our offenders "in their place." These heated and imaginary conversations feel like reality as we use an intimidating pitch and tone of voice. In our misguided passion, we never miss a detail of the offense, as we're purposeful in not allowing the one who hurt us off the hook without adequate retribution.

Not only do we replay every hurtful word or action, but we're also quick to embellish and dramatize. We boldly claim, "If she says_____, then I will respond with _____!" Running ahead of reality, we put words in others' mouths, while working up our emotions in anger without even knowing what their response will be. Not only are we good at embellishing and dramatizing but we tell these stories over and over, embedding them deeper and deeper in our minds and hearts, ultimately keeping us a prisoner to our own game.

When I was in high school and college, I was a good mental storyteller. While I was not verbalizing it aloud, in my mind I replayed the events and words that once pierced my heart. I could recall the details of the incident, who said the words, where we were and what we were doing. At times, I even mentally verbalized arrows I wish I had shot back at them. I could recall the events of the third grade, even first grade if I really desired. As early as I aimed, I could go back and tell detailed events of the words that hurt me the most.

The problem, though, is if we continually think of the wrongs done against us, we're still holding on. What we think about most often reveals where our heart is. If I'm constantly thinking about the wrongs done to me or imagining heated conversations with those who have offended me, I haven't truly forgiven and allowed myself to move on. This is not to say that we will completely forget the past. But in forgiveness, the past no longer is the center of our present-day experience; but rather, our minds are set on Christ.

By compiling and mentally recording all of the wrongs done to us, we gain a false sense of power, control, and superiority. In our self-righteous attitude, our hearts become hardened. We see the speck of sin in others' eyes and miss the plank in our own.[2] The key to forgiving others is being humble enough to recognize that we ourselves have done our fair share of offenses and are in desperate need of forgiveness.

When I Need Forgiveness

It wouldn't be fair to pull the victim card during my elementary and junior high days and fail to recognize my own shortcomings. Just as others have spoken hurtful words to me, I'm accountable for the words that I speak to others, including my own family.

It was a summer evening. My oldest brother and I were playing outside, jumping over a large hole in the ground that had two cement barriers on each side. Having a blast, I don't recall what set me off; but in a moment, I became extremely mad at him. Whether it was the usual conflicts of kids not sharing or an accidental push or nudge during rough play, turning to him in anger I yelled, "You have a flat nose!"

While most of the ridiculous things I have said as a child are somewhat comical to me today, this comment still rings as a sobering moment. Out of all the words I could've used to express my frustrations, why did I choose to make fun of his cleft lip and palate? I knew firsthand what it felt like to be picked on for something I couldn't control. Yet in my anger, I called him the very words that had struck me to the core.

While it's true that *hurting people hurt people*, I learned an additional lesson that day: *sinful* people hurt people. In our sinful nature, we do the very things we don't want to do. We become the person we never wanted to become. As much as it's inevitable that we will need to forgive others, it's inevitable that we ourselves will need to humbly ask for forgiveness.

The Apostle Peter experienced the forgiveness of Christ first hand. After being told he couldn't go with Christ to his crucifixion, Peter boldly and confidently proclaimed he was ready to die for Christ.[3] Jesus replied, "Die for me? I tell you the truth, Peter- before the rooster crows tomorrow morning, you will deny three times that you even know me."[4] As most know, Simon Peter did the very thing he *vowed* he would never do. As Jesus foretold, Peter denied Him three times.[5]

Too often, we only remember Peter for his denials. If we stop reading at his failure, however, we miss a beautiful picture of Christ's redemption and forgiveness. Appearing to Peter for the first time after His death and resurrection, we get a sweet glimpse into the heart of Jesus as He converses with His friend.

Rather than confront him and immediately call him out for his denials, Jesus asked Peter,

"Simon son of John, do you love me more than these?"

Peter answered, "Yes, Lord, you know I love you."

Jesus replied, "Then feed my lambs."

Again, Jesus repeated the question: "Simon son of John, do you love me?"

"Yes, Lord," Peter responded, "you know I love you."

"Then take care of my sheep," Jesus said.

Again. He asked a third time. "Simon son of John, do you love me?"

Hurt that Jesus asked the question three times, Peter said, "Lord, you know everything. You know that I love you."[6]

Jesus asked Peter if he loved Him three times, the equivalent of the number of times that Peter denied Him. This wasn't a coincidence. Each time He commissioned him to feed Christ's sheep. In other words, Jesus was telling Peter, "Your failure didn't disqualify you; I still need you to teach and care for my people." Although Peter failed, he still had faith and commitment to Christ. Even in his failings, Peter still had an assignment, a purpose and was still useful for the kingdom of God.

This beautiful reinstatement by Jesus was not Peter's first lesson in forgiveness. Before his public denials, Peter and Jesus had already discussed the subject. While learning from Jesus as His disciple, Peter asked, "Lord, how often should I forgive someone who sins against me? Seven times?"[7] Peter's suggestion of forgiving seven times seemed generous, so Jesus' response was shocking.[8] "No, not seven times," Jesus replied, "but seventy times seven!"[9]

Not one time. Not seven times. It was not Jesus' intention to give a mere number of 490 times for forgiveness. Peter was sitting in Christ's classroom learning we should forgive others with the limitless and free grace that God forgives us.[10] In this moment, his mind was educated about forgiveness. However, with his personal reinstatement after denying Jesus, Peter *experienced* the limitless and free grace he had once heard about. In Christ's reinstatement after his failures, the lesson was no longer sketched on the chalkboard, but leapt off and penetrated Peter's heart. At that moment, Peter was standing in the reality, experiencing firsthand what it means to be completely forgiven by Jesus Christ.

When I recall my failings in the words I spoke to my brother that summer evening, I cannot help but rejoice in the grace of God in my own life. Rather than grab another by the throat and demand he or she pay me back a few measly pennies, I see the *magnitude* of sin I myself have been forgiven.[11]

From Peter's life, we learn he was a man who loved Jesus yet was in process of growing in maturity and wisdom in Christ. Peter hadn't arrived at perfection.

Neither have I.

Neither have those who have hurt me in the past.

In humility, we recognize that we're in process of growth. *No one has arrived.*

"You have a flat nose!" Oh, how much I need forgiveness! Like Peter, grace and mercy are no longer mere words written on the pages of my Bible; rather, I have *experienced* it firsthand. Considering the immense grace, which the Lord has poured over my own life, I freely extend that same grace to those who have hurt me in the past.[12] Released of my own debt, I *choose* to release my offenders of theirs.

As we walk out our journey with Christ, we will fail and others will fail us. We will falter. We will need picked back up. Like Peter, we may do the very thing that we vowed we would never do. With pure intentions, we desire to be faithful, yet we're still unfaithful at times. We try not to say hurtful words, yet we do. These failings should not elicit condemnation, but should exhort us to examine our hearts, our motives, and answer the question, "Do we truly love Christ?" If the answer is "Yes, Lord, I love you" then in Christ, we repent and move forward. In His forgiveness, we're unbound by our past as we walk in new beginnings and mercies each morning.[13]

CHAPTER 2

Removing the Label

"Though we are incomplete, God loves us completely. Though we are imperfect, He loves us perfectly. Though we may feel lost and without compass, God's love encompasses us completely... He loves every one of us, even those who are flawed, rejected, awkward, sorrowful, or broken."

- Dieter F. Uchtdorf

"Remember who you are. Don't compromise for anyone, for any reason. You are a child of the Almighty God. Live that truth."

- Lysa Terkeurst

Label makers are fun. Type in the name. Tear off the sticker. I can give a label to almost everything I own. There are benefits of a label maker. It helps organize our stuff and makes it easy to find. Putting a label on our luggage helps us find it easily after exiting the plane. A label prevents others from accidently taking our belongings off the rotating belt. Labels on objects can save us unnecessary stress. Even personal nametags are of benefit. Wearing a nametag at a meet and greet helps others remember our names. In these situations, labels are great. However, labeling with hurtful words is painful.

Flat nose.

The name became a label. It felt like a giant sticker on my forehead. Even after forgiving those who called me names, "flat nose" was still the main adjective I used to describe my physical appearance. It's easy to define ourselves by our physical makeup. It's also incredibly burdensome. Identifying by what others think of us leaves us feeling *lesser than* as we fail to measure up to their standard.

Although there are many stories in the Bible that teach us we aren't alone in our feelings of inadequacy, God has used the story of Mephibosheth to reach me in recent years—and teach me that my heart was not much different from those who have gone before me. It's not a story I heard often, but it's a powerful one.

Mephibosheth was the son of Jonathan and the grandson of King Saul. Although Saul started out as a righteous king, he soon grew corrupt. Regretting making Saul king, God vowed that David would take his place.[1] Threatening his kingship, Saul attempted to kill David on multiple occasions. Fearing for his life, David fled and sought assistance from his best friend Jonathan. In response to Jonathan's pledge to aid his escape, David promised to treat him with the faithful love of the Lord as long as he was alive. Even in Jonathan's death, David promised to continue to care for his family.[2] Sealed with a solemn pact and witnessed by the Lord, each man kept his promise.[3]

After the death of Saul and Jonathan, David became the king of Israel.[4] Sometime into his kingship, David recalled his covenantal promise to show God's kindness to Jonathan's family. Desiring to fulfill his promise, David inquired of his servant to find out if Jonathan had any family to whom he could express God's kindness. His servant informed David, "There is still a son of Jonathan who is *lame in his feet*."[5]

Wow. He didn't even call him by his first name! *Lame in his feet.*

Is that all he was known for? I mean, did the young man even have a name or did everyone just label him by his physical makeup? Did his inability to walk define who he was? Surely not! We later find out, he does have a name. His name was Mephibosheth.

Wanting to bless him, David sent for Jonathan's son. Upon his arrival, Mephibosheth bowed low to the ground in deep respect, identifying himself as David's servant.[6] David, making good on his promise to treat Jonathan's family with faithful love, responds to Mephibosheth:

> "Don't be afraid!" David said. I intend to show kindness to you because of my promise to your father, Jonathan. I will give you all the property that once belonged to your grandfather Saul and you will eat here with me at the king's table!" (2 Samuel 9:7)

What an amazing invitation! Mephibosheth is gifted all the property that once belonged to his grandfather Saul and is personally invited to sit and dine at the king's table! David has given the grand invitation and now we eagerly await Mephibosheth's response:

> Mephibosheth bowed respectfully and exclaimed, "Who is your servant, that you should show such kindness to a *dead dog like me*?" (2 Samuel 9:8)

What?! A dead dog? What kind of response is that? A "dead dog" was a Hebrew expression for an "embarrassing piece of garbage."[7] "In Jewish cultures, dogs were detestable, unclean scavengers."[8] "A piece of garbage" is how Mephibosheth saw himself. Like many of us, Mephibosheth had trials in his own life that may have made him question his value and worth.

To understand Mephibosheth's response, we must consider his life situation. At five years of age, Mephibosheth's nurse dropped him while fleeing after the death of Saul and Jonathan, leaving him crippled in both feet.[9] With his physical impairment, even bowing before the king would have been a challenging task. He was a forgotten member of Jonathan's family, as David had to ask if Jonathan still had any living family. His very name, Mephibosheth, means "from the mouth of shame."[10]

Mephibosheth called himself a "dead dog" because he believed he was not worthy or good enough. Maybe it was comments from others that made him feel unworthy. Possibly in his circumstance, Mephibosheth told himself the lie that he was a piece of garbage long enough that he *actually believed it.* Maybe he felt the need to tell King David what was "wrong" with him before being found out. Like, *I'm going to beat you to the punch and make fun of myself before you do. That way it won't hurt so badly.*

Although this story happened thousands of years ago, it amazes me how we can still relate so much today. Mephibosheth labeled himself a piece of garbage. I accepted the label of *flat nose*. It was a challenge to finally tear it off.

He Sees What I Fail to See

One of the biggest reasons we unwittingly accept the labels given to us by others is because we fail to see ourselves the way God sees us. Growing up a huge tomboy, I loved jeans and t-shirts. I spent all my free time playing outside with the boys. Playing soccer each recess, green grass and brown dirt stains became the Hallmark colors embedded upon *all* my blue jeans. While some purchase jeans with holes in them, I earned mine, occasionally snagging my pants while climbing trees with my brother. The only shade of pink found on me were my rosy cheeks as I sweated profusely from running outside for hours.

My sister enjoyed wearing elegant dresses and pretending to sip from her teacup as she headed off to the royal ball. I didn't have the time nor the manners for tea. But more than anything, I disliked wearing dresses. No, I *despised* wearing dresses. Each time my mom mandated that I wear one, I ran and hid from her. Every instance resulted in World War III. When the battle concluded, I looked pretty as ever in my pink little dress, soaked with tears as I sat sulking from the hard fought battle I had lost. The battles continued through much of my childhood. It was not until my early twenties that I started wearing dresses on my own accord. It took almost eight years to stop hearing comments from people who were shocked to see me wearing a dress.

I was a tomboy through and through, and my dad's nickname for me was polar opposite of anything I ever wanted to resemble. My dad called me *Princess*. Quite honestly, the nickname never meant anything to me. I mean, who would want to be a princess? That would require wearing a dress and combing your hair. Out of all the nicknames he could have chosen, *Princess* was *so* not me. As I grew older, I thought, "Dad, your princess is wearing grass-stained jeans with holes in them and is heading outside to get dirty."

Now before we continue, let me clarify. My dad was one of the biggest disciplinarians I have ever known. He wasn't raising a prima donna. He made that *very* clear. *Princess* wasn't encouraging the behavior of a stuck-up little girl. There wasn't tolerance for an entitlement mentality. He would never have allowed his little princess to stomp her foot if she didn't get another pony ride.

When my college teammates found out my dad called me Princess, they laughed! They knew it was nothing I desired. In good clean fun, they adopted the nickname, calling me Princess as well. Ensuring I was royalty, they presented me a princess keychain and shower towel that still make me smile today.

Not only did my teammates have fun with the nickname, but I too like to have fun. As an adult, when my dad asks how my day went, in the squeakiest and most entitled voice I can muster, I exclaim, "Princess isn't happy!" His response? A simple smirk and head shake, as he knows that although I joke, his nickname means more to me now than ever before.

Although it took over twenty years, when God started to teach me that I was fearfully and wonderfully made and that He valued me, my nickname became so meaningful to me. *Princess* was clearly not a reference to a spoiled child who received everything she ever desired; it was my dad's way of telling me, "You have value. I see you. You are precious to me." It was during this time that I realized that even when I couldn't see my value and worth, *my father could.* Even when his nickname was met with awkward looks and complete disinterest on my part, he continued to call me as he saw me: *Valuable.*

We all have a father. Some are wonderful examples of our Heavenly Father's love for us. A good earthly father has a wonderful impact on his daughter's life. Yet some fathers have failed us in many ways. Regardless if we had a positive or negative earthly father, those of us in Christ Jesus serve a perfect Father. His love far surpasses them all.

Far better than the worst dads.

Far better than even the *best* dads.

As my father continued to demonstrate that he saw me and found me valuable, even when I did not see it, our Heavenly Father does this in perfect form. Even when we don't feel worthy and can't see and comprehend the miracle and gift that we are, God stands steadfast and calls us as He *knows* us: His masterpiece.[11] Completely forgiven through Christ Jesus.[12] Greatly loved.[13] His treasured possession.[14]

Anchored in Truth

Even knowing how much God values me, at times, my old friend *insecurity* rears its ugly head. When the old label of *flat nose* takes center stage, I have a choice to stop giving it the brightest spotlight. Whatever I give way to most often will lead me. While our emotions and feelings do matter, they are not our compass. While feelings in and of themselves are not bad, they cannot replace the truth of what God says about us, so we must be careful.

There comes a time as we mature in Christ that we have to make a decision that we will no longer act on what we think or feel or what others have said about us. Rather, we choose to act and walk in the truth about what God has said. Sometimes I *feel* ugly. Sometimes I *feel* unloved. While I may have felt these things, they are not truth.

We cannot allow our emotions to speak louder than truth.

I may *feel* ugly yet I choose to stand on the truth that no matter how I feel, God says that I am fearfully and wonderfully made.[15]

I may *feel* unlovable, yet I choose to replace that lie with the truth that God loves me so much that He calls me His child.[16]

I may *feel* helpless and fearful, yet I choose to anchor on the truth that the One who is in me is greater than he who is in the world.[17]

I may *feel* unseen, yet I choose to remind myself that God calls me His friend and is so incredibly near that He has filled me with His Spirit.[18]

I may *feel* insignificant and without purpose, yet I choose to meditate on the truth that I was created in Christ Jesus for good works which God prepared beforehand.[19] He has called me to be an ambassador for His Son.[20]

God goes so deep revealing our old thought patterns as we learn His truth of who we are. He is never brash and callous in His digging. He lovingly identifies the chains that hold us down, leading us into the freedom we can only find in Him. Even when we don't feel like it and quickly dismiss His truths, He continues calling us as He sees us, knowing one day that it will all mean the world to us when we comprehend even a small portion of how much He cares for us.

Who Am I That You Are Mindful of Me

Mephibosheth was in disbelief that anyone would come and show kindness to someone like him. A cripple. A self-declared piece of garbage. He did not think he deserved the blessing of anyone, much less a king. In his feelings of lack, he asked David, "Who is your servant, that you would show kindness?" In other words, *who am I* that you would come here and bless a person like me?

Some of us have asked this same question. We feel unworthy and messed up and we find ourselves asking, "Who am I that God would love me?" "Who am I that God would care?" We believe that we will never have anything better than the mud and dungeon we have found ourselves dwelling in. Rather than understanding that David had come to bless him because of a covenant promise he made with Jonathan, Mephibosheth could only see what was wrong with himself.

After a late January basketball game at the University of Toledo, I could feel the weight of disappointment bearing down upon me. Our team was not winning. I wasn't playing well. After a poor performance and losing yet another game, I cleaned up in the locker room and headed out to greet my parents who were waiting for me in the gym. Trying to put a smile on my face, I approached my mom, still feeling the heaviness in my heart, wishing it could be easier. As I grew near her, she stood with a smile on her face and reached out her arms to hug me. I wish I could go back in time and have a do-over on this one. Standing before her and exhausted from trying to hold it in I uttered *"Mom........I am worthless."*

As you could imagine, her smile fell very quickly and her eyes began to tear up. She still hugged me, but I could tell my words crushed her spirit. She loved me dearly and didn't think I was worthless. It broke her heart that I truly thought I was. Looking back, I wish I realized that my mom did not come to the game to see the best player or the winning team.

No.

She came for me.

She came to the game to see her daughter, whom she hadn't seen in a long time as I was away at college. Rather than tell her what I thought of myself, I wish I embraced her hug as her daughter, not a performance-driven athlete. I wish I could go back in time and allow her be my mom who loves me unconditionally.

As my mom did that day, God is waiting with His arms wide open, ready to embrace us with a hug. Instead of running into His arms, we sometimes stop. We withdraw. Rather than listen to who He says we are, we feel the need to tell Him all of our shortcomings and why we're unworthy and undeserving of His perfect love. My mom wanted to come to the game to see her daughter. Our Heavenly Father shows up the same way, without a hidden agenda. Even after our worst performance and failures, He is our Father who wants to wrap us up in His arms.[21] God isn't a bandwagon fan who only loves us for what we offer. God comes *for us* and desires to have a personal relationship with us. God has declared His love for us, and it isn't anything we have earned.

After considering the words that came out of my mouth and the tears that fell from my mom's face, I cannot help but ponder how God felt about those words. In the depth of His heart, He wanted me to see the truth of who I am in Him rather than be deceived by my own feelings of inadequacy and insecurity. He wants me to value myself as He values me. I'm valuable, because He deemed me valuable. I'm loved simply because *He loves me.*

Mephibosheth was not the only person to question why anyone, much less a king, would come to bless someone like himself. Throughout Scripture, others have questioned how God could love us so faithfully and purely, even in our imperfections. Who are we that the God of the Universe would take note of us? Even the Psalmist asked a similar question:

> "What is man that You are *mindful* of him, And the son of man that You visit him?" (Psalm 8:4, NKJV).

The word *mindful* comes from the Hebrew word *zakar*. It means, "To mark or keep in remembrance."[22]

Think about it.

Our Father in heaven *marks* us.

He *always* remembers us.

He sets His heart and *affections* upon us.

It's a mind-blowing concept to understand that, despite the enormous number of people who have ever lived, the Creator of the Universe loves each one of us individually, as His very own. We rest in God's love, knowing His love for every human has never changed from the beginning of time. Before you existed, God loved you. Before the world could tell you that you must offer something to be something, God loved you. Before anyone told you that you must look a certain way, God lavished His love upon you.[23]

We may ask the question of "Who Am I?" in two different tones. At face value it's the same question. However, each tone is very different and results in two different responses to God's love. Drawn by God's love but questioning our own worthiness, we stand at a distance and ask, "Who Am I?" with the belief that we aren't good enough to run into His arms. We certainly don't measure up. We feel unworthy to receive His love. Whether it's our past mistakes or allowing the opinions of others to label us as failures, we minimize or deny His love for us, staying at a distance, afraid to come to the Father.

On the other hand, when contemplating the love of God, we can ask "Who Am I?" with a heart of utter amazement and excitement. The God who created the entire Universe, hung each star, and created billions of other people, cares for us. He knows us each by name. It's this understanding that propels us into the arms of Christ and compels us to know Him more. It's this statement of, "Who Am I?" stated with humility and awe, that becomes more than head knowledge and moves to a rock-solid truth that penetrates our heart.

It's no longer a question of *if* I'm worthy or *if* I measure up.

It isn't a question of *if* I deserve His love.

It's a statement of knowing I *am* inadequate.

Yet, Christ within me is adequate. I have all I need.

The pressure releases as I realize I'm *not* enough.

Yet having Christ within me is enough. He's all I need.

It's a statement of knowing I am *unworthy*.

Jesus Christ *alone* is worthy. He is due all praise, honor, and glory.

Yet in His great love, He chose to die for me and make me His forever.

It's a statement of, "I don't know why you love a person like me, but I'm joyfully overwhelmed that you do!" In this state, we no longer question whether we deserve the love of God. We have already determined that we don't. Yet gratitude wells within us knowing He chooses to love us despite ourselves.

Tearing off the Labels

"I am worthless." It was another label. My peers did not give me this one. This time, I created my own. I do this more than I care to admit. I wasn't only wearing the label of flat nose. I added plenty of labels myself. These labels are heavy. These labels are…..false.

They are not my identity.

I'm *done* with old labels. I have worn them long enough. I refuse to define myself by them any longer. One by one, slowly pulling the corner, with a giant rip the labels tear free from the skin, leaving the sting from the glue that once held them *so* secure. It's not that I'm against labels. Remember? Not all labels are bad. I just want the *correct* labels.

When planting my new rosebush, I searched my flowerbeds for the perfect spot. I wanted to plant it in a place that was aesthetically appealing. Most importantly, I ensured that the soil was adequate to sustain and nourish the plant. When I found dry and unfertile soil, I continued searching. I sought out soil that would support the plant's root system and help the plant thrive. Once I found soil that I trusted to support the plant's life, I planted it in the ground. The roots began to *grow*.

In God's love, we have found the richest, full of life giving soil in which to grow our roots. We need not look to another to satisfy. Just as we trust good soil to nourish our plants, we can trust God's love to support, sustain, and nourish our own lives. If we want our roots to grow deep and uphold the plant, we have to remain anchored in the abundant soil of God's love. Knowing we are His, we become *rooted*. Like a massive oak tree, our roots go deep and stretch far into the love of God. Abiding in Him, we entangle and twist our roots so tightly around His love, never being uprooted.

Grounded and settled in God's love, I have a new label.

My new label?

Loved by God.

Unconditionally.

Forever.

This one is *permanent*.

His love is not a halfhearted commitment, which is here today and gone tomorrow.

No. His love is everlasting.

God loves me.

God loves *you*.

Surpassing head knowledge, His love invades our hearts to a degree that our minds cannot fully comprehend. It's final. Permanently embedded deep within our hearts; *we are fully and completely loved by God.*

Just as Mephibosheth was given a seat at the king's table to enjoy a fine feast on a daily basis, we too are invited to the King of king's table. We need not stand at a distance from the Lord. He desires we come near to Him. He stands at the door of our hearts knocking, ready to come in and share a meal as friends.[24] This shared meal "symbolizes acceptance, deep friendship and a covenant relationship."[25]

Unlike an earthly king who demands service at his own table and lords over the people, King Jesus chose to come as a servant, giving His life as a ransom. Unlike today where only the rich and famous enter the king's gates, Jesus invites *all*. Even those who have no social status and who cannot repay Him. He invites those with sin to repent and sit at the table of His salvation.[26] No longer standing at a distance; we accept the invitation to come near to Him. We no longer wonder if we are pretty, smart, or athletic enough. We no longer have to ask the question "Who Am I?" for we have found our *answer in Him*.

CHAPTER 3

The Power of Words

"O Lord, keep our hearts, keep our eyes, keep our feet, and keep our tongues."

- William Tiptaft

"A tongue has no bones but is strong enough to break a heart. So be careful with your words."

- Author Unknown

Shy. If you were to ask my mom to use one word to describe my social skills during my preschool and elementary years it would easily be *shy.* I was so shy; when Webster's Dictionary was looking for the definition of "wall flower," they simply put my picture next to the word, as no further explanation was required.

I took being shy to a completely new level as I *never* wanted to leave my mom's side. Everywhere she went, I wanted to go. If she went to the grocery store, I promised not to ask her to buy me anything if she took me along. If she agreed to bring me to the dentist with her, I promised to sit in the waiting room quietly and not complain. Even when she tried slow-dancing with my dad at weddings, I was there trying to cut in on the dance! I wanted to go *everywhere*. Nothing was off limits. If she hadn't shut the door in my face, I would have followed her into the bathroom as well!

Much to my mom's credit, I wasn't an easy child to raise. Being shy, I seldom spoke to anyone other than my family. As I grew older, I became more willing to speak to others but still limited my conversation. I would never say more than was required of me. In middle school, our church transitioned to a new pastor. The first time she asked my name, she mistakenly thought I said, "Daisy." So each Sunday morning she greeted me with, "Good Morning, Daisy." Never once correcting her that my name was Stacey, my simple reply was, "Good Morning." To no fault of her own, she called me Daisy for years and was genuinely surprised when she learned that it wasn't my name.

One of the funniest memories occurred when I played on a summer softball team with my older sister. In true preteen girl fashion, my teammates liked to be loud and rambunctious, reciting cheers from the dugout to encourage our teammates who were on the playing field. Using homemade drumsticks, made of a sawed off golf club handle with a golf ball duct-taped to the end, the leader beat a rhythm on an old kitty litter box as the girls became fired up and cheered on the team.

If the pitcher threw a wild pitch that hit the dirt, the girls immediately cheered, "Rollin' Rollin' Rollin' pitchers going bowlin', get those worms some helmets!"

If my teammates wanted to intimidate the other team by showing how tough they were, they would chant (To the tune of "I Don't Know What I've Been Told"):

"We don't wear no miniskirts. We just wear our softball shirts!"

"We don't drink no lemonade. We just drink our Gatorade!"

"We don't play with Barbie dolls. We just play with bats and balls!"

"Sound off…1..2…..Sound off…3…4"

Although I desperately wanted to participate on the softball team, I had no desire to participate in these cheers. Each inning my teammates cheered as I stood without saying a word. After many games of refusing to participate in the cheers, a few of my teammates pulled my sister aside and asked, "Does she talk at all?" Without missing a beat my sister replied, "Well yeah, she doesn't stop talking at home!!" Obviously, I was horrified! How dare she tell them I can speak!?

Although I did not appreciate my sister calling me out, I have to admit, she was telling the truth. Although I refused to participate in the cheers in front of my teammates, when I got home, I drove my sister nuts, running around the house loudly chanting my favorite cheer. Acting as if I was a batter about to get a big hit, I obnoxiously cheered at the top of my lungs, "Hit it, rip it, knock it around. *Knock that pitcher off the mound!*"

Back in the dugout for the next game, I sat in my usual "I refuse to speak in public" silence. My sister was up to bat and our team needed a big hit. Fired up, my teammates started my favorite cheer; the one they had done many times before: "Hit it, rip it, knock it around. Knock that pitcher off the mound!" With the crack of the bat, the ball propelled directly at the pitcher. Smacking her square in the stomach, she fell over in intense pain. The hit was so fierce that the stitches of the softball imprinted upon her stomach. To everyone's shock, my sister literally knocked the pitcher off the mound!

The next time our team needed a big hit, the girls roared the chant one more time. "Hit it, rip it..." In his wisdom, the coach suddenly interrupted, "Girls, maybe we shouldn't be saying that chant. You remember what happened last time, don't you?" The coach recognized the *power of our words.* Although he probably didn't realize it, he taught me that our words have impact.

Impacting Words

The power of our words are undeniable. Just yesterday, while observing a little girl with a birth defect swinging on the monkey bars with her peers, I couldn't help but recognize the impact of hurtful words. As the child played so carefree with the other children, seeming completely oblivious to their differences, I thought, "She has no idea that she was born with a birth defect and neither do any of the other children."

What is it that makes us first realize we are different from others? At an early age, most of us learned we were different because *someone told us we were.* In our early childhood, differences were noticed less or weren't interpreted as a *negative* thing. In just a few short years, though, we hear the opinions of others and now these words begin to form our identity of who we believe we are. This is the power of hurtful words.

Although our identity can be negatively shaped by hurtful words, the life-giving words of others can change our lives for the better. Although the words were not spoken directly to me, there was one story that always encouraged my heart as it taught me the power of only a few life-giving words. My favorite story comes from Mary Ann Bird, a woman who was born in 1928 with a severe cleft lip and palate. She was also deaf in one ear. She was born before corrective surgery was readily available and her classmates teased her without mercy. Bird's unpublished memoir, *The Whisper Test*, is now used as a powerful sermon illustration around the world:

> One of the worst experiences at school, she reported, was the day of the annual hearing test. The teacher would call each child to her desk, and the child would cover first one ear, and then the other. The teacher would whisper something to the child like "The sky is blue" or "You have new shoes." This was "The Whisper Test." If the teacher's phrase was

heard and repeated, the child passed the test. To avoid the humiliation of failure, Mary Ann would always cheat on the test, secretly cupping her hand over her one good ear so that she could still hear what the teacher said.

One year Mary Ann was in Miss Leonard's class, one of the most beloved teachers in the school. Every student, including Mary Ann, wanted to be noticed by her, wanted to be her pet. Then came the day of the dreaded hearing test. When her turn came, Mary Ann was called to the teacher's desk. As Mary Ann cupped her hand over her good ear, Miss Leonard leaned forward to whisper.

"I waited for those words," Mary Ann wrote, "which God must have put into her mouth, those seven words which changed my life." Miss Leonard did not say, "The sky is blue" or "You have new shoes." What she whispered was, "I wish you were my little girl."[1]

In the busyness of life, rather than just seeing the *task* of many hearing screens, Miss Leonard saw a little girl who needed an encouraging word. Those simple seven words inspired Mary Ann and changed her life forever. As Mary Ann cupped her good ear to avoid the embarrassment of failing yet another hearing test, her teacher had to realize that the test results were skewed. Likely sensing Mary Ann's frustration, Miss Leonard saw *past* whether or not she could hear a whisper and just simply spoke the words loud enough that she knew Mary Ann *needed to hear*.

This remains one of my favorite stories because it reminds me that it's not the quantity of words but the quality of the words that have a powerful and lasting impact. Working as a Speech-Language

Pathologist, this story reminds me that no matter how routine a day seems to me, each moment is an opportunity to see the child more than the task that needs completed and speak life-giving words to the children I serve.

God Works in Awkwardness

Just as words changed Mary Ann's life, I have also been on the receiving end of genuine and kind words that encouraged my heart. Some words made an immediate impact, while other words were called to remembrance years later, making an equal impact at that time. These words helped me realize the lies I had believed about myself and helped me see myself in a brand new way.

Before eating a meal at a local restaurant with my college teammates, I went to the bathroom to wash my hands. Leaning forward over the sink, a woman quickly tapped me on the shoulder. Before I turned completely around, she quickly blurted out, "You are beautiful. I have a niece with a cleft lip and palate, and I want you to know you're beautiful." Caught by surprise, I muttered, "Um… OK." She quickly jetted out the door.

Without a doubt, the interaction was incredibly awkward. However, with time I have been able to look past the awkwardness of the very quick exchange and see a woman who actually understood my struggle: the struggle to believe I was beautiful.

Having a niece with a cleft lip and palate, she understood my situation more than most. It was her heart's desire that her niece and I know that we were not mistakes. I appreciate this woman and wish I had better words to express my gratitude in that moment. Now, having nieces of my own and desiring that they would know and anchor their identity in Christ, I can see beyond the awkwardness of the moment. I'm now grateful that this complete stranger saw beyond herself and took a moment to try to encourage my heart. If I could go back in time, I would thank her and tell her I appreciate her stepping out of her comfort zone in attempts to speak life-giving words to me. Not knowing what my response would be, she moved past her fear of awkwardness to show genuine care, no matter how uncomfortable it made her.

I cannot help but wonder if she walked away; possibly feeling like a failure because of my lame response. I cannot help but wonder if she walked away feeling awkward but offered a prayer on my behalf. I wonder if she prayed that one day I would no longer be ashamed of my cleft lip and palate and no longer believe the lie that I was ugly. Maybe she looked past the cleft and prayed that God would do a work within my heart to teach me to see myself as He saw me. Maybe she was not sure what to pray, so she simply asked God that *He do His work* in my life.

Nearly fifteen years after my interaction with the woman in the bathroom, an elderly woman approached me at a friend's wedding and said, "I hope you don't mind, but I notice you have a cleft lip and palate." The words that once made me cringe and want to hide no longer served as a banner over my head that screams, "Yes, I have an issue!" Rather, these words now served as an invitation to acknowledge that while I was born with a cleft lip and palate, God created us to grow together and share our hearts with one another.

This elderly woman continued to share how she had a daughter with a cleft. She shared of how she became a Christian and what God had done in her heart since she experienced the love of Christ. She encouraged me on my journey and rather than feel I was the odd one out, I truly felt as if somehow this complete stranger and I understood each other and just did a small yet very meaningful part of life together.

I see so clearly now how God uses it all. He uses the moments we feel that we risked, failed, and were misunderstood. I believe God uses it all. If not today, another day. Behind every changed life, someone risked awkwardness. It takes a simple step of faith to offer the Gospel or a word of encouragement, and we don't truly understand the impact that God is making through us. Even when it does not feel like a grand and life-changing moment, may we have the courage to play even the smallest roles to help build encouragement within others. Like my instance in the bathroom, the moment may even feel like a failed opportunity. However, we have to remember that our words may resonate days or even years later. Truly, the roles that often appear the smallest and insignificant are sometimes the most profound and life-changing.

Even though I don't know her name, I'll never forget the woman in the restroom. This woman risked. She pushed. She raised the bar for me. She helped pull this wallflower from the wall. She will never know the full impact that her words had on me that day. No longer do I see words as something to fear or hide from; I now understand that words are a *gift* from our Creator. Language is a precious gift because we can give life through our words.

In time, her words brought me healing and peace.[2] Understanding that our words can help the hurting, I no longer want to allow fear to stop me from speaking life-giving words to others. How many times had I not offered encouraging words for fear that my words might not come out right or that I may be misunderstood? How many times did I remain silent because I was overly concerned about what others may think of me? As the woman did that day, I want to use my words to bring hope to others. When prompted by the Holy Spirit to speak, I want to speak. With His help, not a word will be wasted.

Learning to Speak Kindly to Myself

Although grateful for the improvements that had been made over the years, I still found myself hoping that with each consecutive surgery, my cleft lip and palate would be less and less noticeable. When the physical repair was complete, only occasionally would a child or adult ask about the scars on my lip. Yet, long after the hurtful comments dissipated and others no longer mentioned my cleft lip and palate, I still struggled with my appearance.

Looking back, I realized that I still struggled at times because, although my external appearance had been repaired, *my mind and heart hadn't been repaired and retrained to think like Christ*. My external appearance was mended but my internal condition hadn't been healed. I could have all the surgeries in the world to repair the cleft lip and palate; but if I didn't renew my mind to think like Christ, I would always believe lies more than truth.

Thinking back to the awkward exchange of the woman in the restroom, I wondered why it took me almost fifteen years to see that her words were true. Maybe the words were hard to receive because they came from a complete stranger. While that does make it a little different, I cannot help but recall the number of times I asked God to have someone else, someone besides my parents, say that I was beautiful. As a teenager, I always thought my mom and dad had to say nice things to me. I told God that if those words came from someone else, someone who didn't *have* to say it, then I would truly believe it.

I think we have all been there. God uses someone to speak truth into our lives; but we pause and hesitate, justifying that even though it's truth, we want to hear it from someone who didn't have to say it. God in His kindness sent someone else to say those words to me. There I stood, the words came, but I didn't believe them. Just awkwardness and walking away. What would it take for me to believe the words?

I couldn't receive her words right away because those words were so foreign to any of the words that I was speaking to myself. I was not speaking kindly to myself, so why would I listen when others did? What I find contradictory about how women speak to themselves is that, if we're honest, we probably speak far worse about ourselves than we would anyone else. We say negative things about ourselves that we would *never* say to another person. I cannot remember the last time I called someone else *stupid*, but it wasn't that long ago that

I called myself those very words. I truly don't know anyone who I think is ugly, yet it's a word that I would freely use to describe myself.

To learn to speak properly to ourselves, we must be diligent about what thoughts enter our minds and hearts. Out of the abundance of our heart, the mouth speaks.[3] What we treasure in our hearts and think in our minds will come out of our mouths. When learning to speak to ourselves, we should desire that the words of our mouths would be pleasing to God.[4] We should speak as though we were speaking the words of Jesus and ask that He guard our lips.[5] If I know that Jesus would never say that I'm ugly, dumb, or unlovable, then why would I?

In order to ensure we're thinking and speaking truth, we must *guard* our minds. In guarding our minds, we learn that every thought that attempts to pass through the gate of our mind is subject to the approval of God. As a word passes into our minds, we have the option to accept or reject it. When the thought isn't of God, rather than continually thinking on it, we can simply *choose another thought*. When the thought doesn't line up with God's Word, we know our thoughts are wrong because God's Word is never wrong. His Truth never changes, but rather, we are changed.

We must be *mindful* about what we're thinking. Old faulty thought patterns will remain our focus if we're never willing to examine what we're telling ourselves. We must ask ourselves if we believe something because we have told ourselves it long enough or whether we believe it because it's backed by the Word of God? Are we willing to stop and examine the thoughts that enter our minds, or do we quickly and flippantly accept the first words our minds conceive?

While replacing my old green carpet with updated wood flooring, God taught me a lesson on *measuring* and accepting the words that I speak to myself with *careful intention*. As I was preparing to cut a board, I recalled the carpenter's motto to "measure twice, cut once." If I want to save money on the amount of boards I purchase for a project, it's a good idea to not quickly react and cut the board to the first measurement. An intelligent carpenter always measures twice.

Measuring twice requires that I pause and double-check before making the final cut. It's wise to consider twice because once I cut a board, it's *permanent.*

Just like cutting a board, we're wise to *pause and double-check* the words that we speak to ourselves. It can save ourselves unnecessary heartache. When we pause, we ask, "Is it true?" "Does it line up with what God says about me?" Although words are not permanent like cutting a board, it can still be very costly. Words have power to wound deeply and can have a negative effect on our mind and emotions. Knowing this, we cautiously proceed with our words, thinking twice before we take them as truth.

CHAPTER 4

A False Identity Shattered

"A seed has to crack and break to grow."

- Author Unknown

"Brokenness is the stripping of self-reliance and independence from God. The broken person has no confidence in his own righteousness or his own works, but he is cast in total dependence upon the grace of God working in and through him."

- Nancy Leigh DeMoss

It seemed like I was born to play sports. I pretty much came out of the womb throwing a ball. At just three years of age, my oversized ball cap covered my face as I attempted to balance my yellow plastic bat on my shoulder. Extending the well-worn Wiffle ball to my mom, I begged, "Throw me another one." She agreed to throw another pitch, but this would be the last, as it was time to start supper. If it were up to me, we would have never stopped playing. After heading inside while my mom prepared the food, I sat on the kitchen chair as she sporadically threw me the ball in between tasks.

Sure, we both knew the rule of no throwing balls in the house; but dad wasn't home from work yet, and neither of us would tell him.

Turning six years old, I was so excited to play on my first sports team. Although I wasn't entirely sure what t-ball would include, I was told to bring my glove and bat so I knew it must be a good time. Wearing my white baseball pants and red stirrups socks, I was proud to wear a Red Sox uniform. I knew the basics of the game. I needed to keep my eye on the ball when hitting. When playing the field, I was told to keep my glove down and don't let the other team score runs. Half the team was picking daisies and spinning circles while the coach gave his instructions, but he had my full attention. If the goal was to tag the other team out when they ran the bases, well then, that is what I was going to do.

Knees bent and in position, I was ready to field any ball that came my way. With a solid hit off the tee, the ball flew over my position at shortstop and landed into left field. Being equal distance from the ball, the center and left fielders both ran toward the ball laying in the grass. Approaching the ball at the same time, instead of throwing it into the infield, they began wrestling and fighting over the ball! While most thought it was a comical scene to watch, I was mortified. "What are they doing?! The runner is rounding first base and will score while they're too busy fighting!"

Unwilling to lose the game while my teammates rolled on the ground squabbling over the baseball, I sprinted out to left field. Prying the ball from their hands, I turned and ran towards home as the runner was now rounding third base. With ball in glove, I ran as fast as my little legs would carry me to catch the runner before he reached home plate. Just mere feet before reaching home plate, with arms stretched far, I tagged the runner on the back and then dropped the ball out of my glove! The umpire correctly deemed him safe. I was mad.

That was only the foreshadowing of the competitive nature within me.

Whether it was softball or basketball, I loved the game and

always wanted to win. Not only did I have the passion for sports, but as I grew, I developed the athletic body type as well. In middle school, with broad shoulders and a solid frame, I felt most comfortable in my knee-length basketball shorts and cut off t-shirts. The baggier, the better. I was taller, stronger, and weighed more than most girls. My large hands allowed me to palm basketballs in each hand without much effort. My shoe size resembled my brother's more than my sister's. I didn't have a petite bone in my body. I didn't feel feminine.

I certainly never felt pretty.

A Self-Proclaimed Identity, Crushed

Although I struggled with my physical appearance, I felt validated by my ability to play basketball well. My athleticism made me feel as if I did have something to offer this world. Feeling as if I had nothing else to offer, my passion for sports became my worth and identity. I worked hard to be a better basketball player, falsely believing that becoming a good athlete granted me value, despite a few of my peers' opinions of me.

It was very easy to find my worth and identity in basketball. Believing the lie that I was only as good as I preformed, I measured my value and acceptance in wins and losses and overall athletic performance. In my head, it was easy to compute; if I played a good game, then I was valuable and worthy of attention, admiration, and love. If I did not perform well, I was unworthy, invaluable, and undeserving of love.

When I didn't play well, I sulked in disappointment. There were sleepless nights, tossing and turning, as my game performance left me restless and not measuring up to my personal standards. I know, you're thinking, "Wow, that's pretty extreme, Stacey." You're correct. I can see that now. Nevertheless, when in the midst, it seemed very rational, and I truly believed it. I grasped at basketball to ensure myself I did have something to offer.

I bought one of the biggest lies of my identity days before my last high school basketball game. Cooling down from an intense practice, my teammates and I lined up to finish off the practice with free throws. As we were shooting, a teammate casually mentioned a recent newspaper article that highlighted our latest victory. In a joking manner, she jabbed me for being mentioned in the headline of the article. Leaning towards me she said, "You may get all the basketball recognition, but I get all the boys." Without blinking an eye or thinking twice, I fully agreed with her. "That's right," I thought, "God hasn't made me pretty, but at least He made me athletic. The boys will *never* be interested in me, but at least I'm good at basketball. I *always* will have basketball."

I tore my ACL the next game.

Sometimes life feels like a sucker-punch in the gut. Life hits and knocks the air right out of us. What once felt like a smooth sailing ship bound for paradise now had hit bumpy waters, leaving us battered and unsteady. My senior year of high school felt much like that. At the start of my final high school basketball season, the year held much promise and hope. Just five games into the young season, our team was undefeated, ranked in the state, and I was quickly nearing the 1,000-point scorer's club.

This was the time.

All those pick-up games in the driveway, endless defensive and offensive drills in the gym, and all the late-night shooting practices led me to this moment. Taking a large early lead in our sixth game of the season, it was simply one of those games where everything was clicking. I was firing on all cylinders. The rim seemed as big as an ocean, and anywhere I threw the ball, it was going to go in.

As I had done a million times before, with the ball in my possession, dribbling to the basket, I came to a jump stop. After gathering myself to shoot, I took a large leap in the air. As I landed, my right knee buckled beneath me. Collapsing to the ground, the ball rolled out of bounds. Quickly pulling myself up off the floor, I hobbled over to the bench area. I knew something was wrong.

I never suffered a significant injury before in my life. Sitting on the bench as the athletic trainer assessed my knee, I had no idea that I would never play another high school basketball game. MRI testing at the local hospital revealed I tore my ACL. Surgery was required to repair. Prematurely, my senior basketball season was over.

To some, no longer being able to play basketball would be irrelevant. However, to my 18-year-old self, basketball was my self-proclaimed purpose in this life. My lifelong dreams were *broken*. They were *shattered*. *I* was shattered.

My dream of being a thousand-point scorer: *Gone*.

My dream of my teammates and I competing for a state championship: *Gone*.

My dream of winning the conference championship my senior year: *Gone*.

In the midst of broken dreams, it's difficult to see clearly. Although in the moment my understanding was bleak, with time and healing, I have been able to see more plainly. I have better understood the situation. See, what *I* desired most was gone. However, what seemed like a dream failed was actually the amazing freedom of a *false identity* crushed. The tearing of my ACL was a blessing in disguise as I traded my false identity of being a performance-driven athlete with the truth that my identity and value is found in Christ alone.

For this reason, I'm now grateful for my season-ending ACL tear.

In my limited earthly thinking, I would have loved a wonderful athletic career, free of injury, obstacles, and failure. However, without a doubt, the tearing of my ACL was the launching point from which *God opened my eyes and ears to who I was in Christ*. For this, I'm eternally grateful. Sidelined from the sport I loved, I still believed I was not pretty, but I no longer had basketball to create a sense of validation or worth. With a torn ACL, I was no longer a basketball player. So who was I? Just a girl born with a cleft lip and palate? Is that all I was? I was at a crossroad. Was I going to exchange one false identity for another? Would I no longer label myself a basketball player, something I thought I was good at—only to transfer my identity back to my cleft, the one thing I perceived was wrong with me?

Without basketball, for the first time in my life, I felt like I had nothing of value to offer. With nothing in my hands to offer, at the feet of Jesus, is where I found peace. Eternal purpose. Restoration. *True love.* A far better love than all the boys in the world could ever give. When basketball (the one thing that I thought I couldn't live without) was removed, I learned that in reality there was only One in whom I couldn't live without.

His name is *Jesus.*

With false identities now removed, I could finally see that a deep and personal relationship with Jesus Christ was all that mattered. I no longer comforted myself with the lie that, "Well, God hasn't made me pretty; but at least He made me athletic." I recognized this lie and realized there was only one statement I needed to remind myself:

The God of the Universe made me *His.*

A Value that Never Changes

I wish I could claim that I never again doubted my value and worth apart from Christ. Even after the repairing of my ACL and beginning my college basketball career, there were still times when I made sports my main identity and value.

During my sophomore year of college, it was time to declare my major. After going back and forth on multiple options, I still had no idea what I wanted to do. I was beginning to experience burn out with sports; however, I couldn't even fathom that maybe God had something different for me than the sport I had known my entire life. Without knowing what I wanted to do, I decided to do the same thing I have *always* done. A sports management degree was my choice; after all, sports were who I thought I was.

Later that year, my college friends and I made plans to go out to eat with all of our parents after my upcoming basketball game. On a rare occasion that all of our parents were visiting the same weekend, my friends thought it would be fun to all hang out. However, on the day of the game, I didn't play well. After the game, they were excited to hang out, but I declined because I didn't feel like I deserved to go.

The following year, during a close competitive match-up, the game was coming down to the wire. With seconds left, I secured a rebound underneath our basket and had an opportunity to win the game with an uncontested shot within mere feet of the basket. Seconds after the ball released from my hand, clinking off the backboard the buzzer sounded signaling the end of the game.

I missed the shot.

We lost.

With the weight of the world on my shoulders, I struggled the rest of that Saturday and went to church the next day. At that church service, I learned that nothing I accomplish or fail at in this world could change my value and worth in Him.

I could make or miss the shot.

In God's eyes, it changed nothing in regards to how much He loved me.

I could make or miss the shot.

God still demonstrated His love for me by sending Jesus to the cross for my sins.

I'm still learning. Even today, this world presents many opportunities for me to grasp at external achievements as my source of value and worth. As the invitation beckons, as I feel the pull towards lesser things, I recall the only One in whom I found *constant* and *unchanging* value and worth: Jesus Christ. Nothing else will ever satisfy. He is where I choose to *remain*.

The Beauty of Brokenness

I have seen God work far more through my brokenness than through the situations that have gone as planned. Brokenness is beautiful because of what God does in the midst—even though we cannot see it at the time. In our brokenness, we find that *God is incredibly near.* We become less, and He becomes our everything.

For me, struggle has brought closer intimacy with my Father. I rejoice—because the intimacy birthed with God during the hardest times of my life has ended up being the same intimacy I continue to enjoy long after the storm has ended. Understanding this and embracing this intimate relationship is a deep treasure that cannot be purchased. The darkest nights develop the strongest bonds.

The tearing of my ACL, for example, brought me a newfound freedom. I was genuinely surprised to find that God had gifted me to do more than play basketball. No longer did I have to continue being involved in sports simply because it was what I had always done. I was free to lay my life into God's hands and ask Him to shape my life for *His purposes.* I asked Him to use me, in whatever capacity and season of my life He had planned.

No longer marked by what we do, we're marked by the Creator to whom we belong. We will wear many different hats in this lifetime. As jobs and God's calling on our lives change, there will always be one constant. We're primarily marked as His beloved. When we identify as being His, we're free to take our death grip off the things we do. We know that even if one season of our life ends, God will open the next chapter. He isn't done with us yet.

Understanding I'm enough in Christ frees me to attempt my dreams. If I fail, paralysis doesn't stop me from trying again. I move forward, knowing that my identity and worth in Christ never changes despite any outcome. Understanding that my value is not dependent on the opinions of others or the results of my latest challenge frees me to offer my best without fear. Anchored, I can face challenges head on. In vulnerability, I can offer my ideas—knowing that even if my ideas are rejected, Christ still loves me the same.

Brokenness is beautiful because it changes how we see ourselves. The tearing of my ACL reminded me that no matter how many points I scored, how many colleges offered me scholarships, or how many people applauded my success, I was a mere fragile clay vessel who *experienced limitations.* In brokenness, we realize that great power only comes from God, not ourselves.[1] Brokenness is beautiful because it becomes more about His will than our own. In our struggles, we find that we are not the solution, nor are we all-knowing and powerful. Arrogance and self-pride. They quickly flee when we realize that we are desperately in need of God.

We give up.

We stop trying to do this life on our own and we fall at the foot of the cross. We don't come to Christ because we think we have all the answers. We certainly don't come to Christ because we think He can learn anything from us. We come to Him broken. Contrite in spirit. Repentant. Knowing we have made it more about our glory than His glory for far too long. We understand we have nothing to offer and are in need of a Savior.

Brokenness is beautiful because in our weakness, Christ becomes our strength.[2] In maturity, although the struggle was not easy and we may never want to experience it again, we can look back and even thank God for the struggle as we realize we're far more God reliant than ever before. When we relinquish control to God, we find new strength in our surrender.

I Can Do All Things

One of my favorite Bible verses is Philippians 4:13. It's one of the most common Scriptures quoted on the field of competition. I recited it too. I may have written it on the soles of my basketball sneakers. I may have worn a few shirts that proclaimed this message:

"I can do *all things* through Christ who strengthens me" (NKJV).

All things! I told myself in the pregame warm-up. Like win a conference championship my senior year. All things! Like win a state championship and set the school scoring record. So what happened? If I could do all things, why did I tear my ACL? I never did accomplish *any* of those things, much less *all* things.

After reading the entire Scripture, I realized that I didn't fully understand the context of the verse at the time. It didn't mean what I thought. When Paul penned those words, he was not competing for a conference title. He wasn't concerned about school records or if he would be a Division II basketball state champion. When Paul penned those words, he was a Roman *prisoner.*

See, Paul and I were talking about different things. I was treating God like Santa Claus, as if His utmost concern was making my senior year go exactly the way I wanted. Paul had far greater insight into the heart of God. Writing from his prison cell, Paul wasn't concerned about avoiding hardship, he was learning to find contentment in the *midst* of his trials. Paul knew what it was like to have plenty. He certainly knew what it was like to lack. He found the secret to living well in *any* circumstance. He found the secret to living well in *all things*: Good. Bad. Ugly.

Paul wasn't saying he would get everything he wanted.

As followers of Jesus Christ, we don't always get everything we desire in this world. ACLs tear. Dreams fail. We're far from getting all things. Our promise is not that the road will always be easy; the promise is that *no matter what,* Jesus Christ will see us through. We *will* face trials in this life. Yet with Christ, we don't have to dread what may come.

We can be truly glad because we know that trials prove our faith genuine. As fire purifies gold, trials purify our faith. No longer praising God just when times are good, we praise God no matter what the challenge. When our faith in Jesus Christ stays strong as we remain in and pass through trials, we can be sure that our faith is genuine.[3]

Before I tore my ACL, it was easy to share my faith in Jesus Christ while on the mountaintop, when things were going as I hoped. However, after I tore my ACL, I found the real measure of the authenticity of my faith occurred in the valley. The test of my faith wasn't how steadfast my walk with the Lord was when *I* was winning, and *I* was doing well. The real test of my faith and my claim to be a follower of Jesus Christ occurred when it was no longer about *me*.

When things fell apart, would I still praise Him? Would I still share of His goodness? Would I sit on the sidelines, cheer on my teammates, and be truly happy for their victories? Or would I sulk? Would I still spend time with the Lord, or would I pull away from Him because I didn't get my way?

Honestly, I didn't handle the tearing of my ACL in the best manner.

I recall the first night I bathed after my surgery. I wanted a bath, but I couldn't do it on my own. My stitches had to stay dry. It was impossible with my leg locked in a restraining brace. I was humiliated that my mom had to help me. I honestly forget why she made me so mad; but as she was trying to help, with anger like a lobster coming out of water, I snapped at her.

Calmly looking back at me, she simply said, "I didn't want this to happen to you."

Silence covered the room.

I knew I was being a jerk.

Only an apology was appropriate.

Can I please get a redo?

Today, I'm still learning to be content in all things. I have learned that life is far bigger than the game of basketball. Most of us will suffer greater losses than a mere basketball game. We will experience greater loss than the tearing of an ACL. We see loved ones suffer. We lose relationships that we have fought hard to keep. Financial hardships strike.

Some will suffer birth defects.

Despite our struggles in this lifetime, we remain in Him. Our present sufferings are small and *will not last forever.*[4] With my cleft lip and palate only being temporary while I'm here on earth, I'm free to take my eyes off the shape of my nose and the scars on my lip and focus on my relationship with Christ. The cleft, which created struggles that will only last a short time on this earth, is never the focus. With my eyes on the cleft, it seems so huge; but with my eyes on eternity, the cleft seems so trivial. Our present sufferings do not compare to what it will be like even after one minute of being in His presence in heaven.

Knowing our present struggles will not last forever, we never give up. In wisdom, we separate and value the things in our lives that will have an eternal impact and make those the utmost priority. We're strengthened when we no longer fret over the things of this world that are here today and gone tomorrow.

My lip, once separated in three pieces from the cleft, retain the scars that remain from the surgical closure of my lip. The scars that I once dreaded, I now see as beautiful as they remind me that *God is healing me.* Each time I look in the mirror and see my scars, God reminds me that He restores broken things. He takes our shattered and broken dreams and uses them for a far greater purpose: revealing our true value and worth in Him alone. God has mended and continues to mend my heart. He can mend yours. Lay the pieces into His hands.

CHAPTER 5

Rejection

"If you live for people's acceptance, you will die from their rejection."

- Lecrae

With great doubts and insecurities, at times I felt completely unseen and overlooked by the opposite sex. Although known for my athletic abilities, I desired to be seen and recognized as beautiful. When playing basketball with the boys on the playground, I occasionally heard them talking about the pretty girls—the girls they had crushes on. The arrows penetrated my heart as I realized these boys *saw* other girls. They recognized and noticed other girls but did not see me in that way.

Eventually when they found out who my sister was, a few of them commented on how pretty she was. My sister frequently received compliments about her looks. I received compliments on my athletic abilities but never had the older women oohing and awing over my beautiful hair, eyes, or my cute button nose.

I share vulnerably, but I know I'm not alone in my feelings of being unseen and overlooked. My sister confides that although she was seen for her physical beauty, she desired to be seen for more than her physical appearance. She often felt overlooked in other areas. We all can relate to feeling unwanted, unchosen, or unseen. It may not be a cleft lip and palate. It could be the size of your waistline, your GPA in high school, or your comfort level in social situations. Regardless of what it is, in one way or another, we all will experience some form of rejection.

Will I Be Chosen?

My dad was looking at the variety of jewelry displayed on the counter as I stood a few feet behind him. I was supposed to be helping him look for a set of earrings to give my mom for Christmas, but something else caught my attention. Behind the counter stood a young woman, who looked like the older version of myself. I was twelve years old. She was in her mid-twenties. Although she was older than I was, we had something in common. She, too, had a bilateral cleft lip and palate.

As she approached my dad to assist him with his purchase, I noticed she wore an engagement ring on her left hand. In the course of conversation, she mentioned she was getting married in a few months.

Married.

Someone chose her.

I don't recall much of the interaction after that point. I just remember thinking, "Well, she has a cleft lip and palate and is getting married; *maybe* I will get married one day as well." It was my first interaction with another female who had a cleft; and I learned that, although the boys on the playground hadn't noticed me yet, maybe one day someone would. Just like someone recognized and chose her. *Just maybe.*

Fast-forward twenty years. I was thirty-two and still single. My hope of maybe getting married was dwindling as fast as my secret stash of Oreo cookies. With my few dating opportunities all failing, the fear of rejection from the opposite sex because of my physical appearance was hitting harder than ever before.

Many well-meaning people offered to set me up on blind dates over the years. A blind date provoked a deep sense of fear. The fear that I wouldn't be accepted because of my cleft paralyzed me at times. Other times, I accepted the invitation to go on a blind date yet feared I might be rejected because I wasn't pretty enough.

One particular blind date I remember vividly. When my sister mentioned, "Hey, there is a guy I think you should meet." With a sense of urgency, I questioned, "Does he know about the scars on my face?" After she informed me that she showed him a picture from my Facebook profile, I wondered if the picture portrayed the reality of my scars.

While enjoying good food and conversation on a first date, we discussed a great variety of topics. We discussed trivial subjects like hobbies and favorite foods. We even touched on some deeper matters of faith. The conversation flowed. His questions were coming straight down the plate, and I was hitting them out of the ballpark. Suddenly, pulling an unexpected question from left field he asked, "May I ask how you got those scars on your lip?"

Although I'm an open book in most regards, the question felt heavy and full of tension. I tried to keep the wrestling within me from revealing itself outwardly through my facial expressions. I felt like I needed to explain myself. I didn't want to discuss the most uneasy and vulnerable topic in my life with someone I just met. The question served as a reminder that I couldn't simply be a "normal" girl on a "normal" date.

To be fair, as much as it hurt, I know he didn't mean harm. Like his other questions, he was just trying to get to know me better. Had he asked about the faded scar above my left eye, I would have enthusiastically shared how I got it in junior high when I ran into a tetherball pole while playing football at recess. Running down field, while looking back over my left shoulder to see the pass from the quarterback, I never saw the pole and hit it so hard it knocked me to the ground! My tone would only drop as I admitted that I didn't catch the ball! Had he asked me about the scar on my right forearm, I would have proudly shared how I cut myself on a rusty nail while jumping over a fence in the barn. Sure, it left a scar; but I cleared the fence easily and did it many times again!

But he didn't ask about those scars. Those injuries were comical to me—they didn't carry an emotional punch like the scars from my cleft. Although the surgical incisions healed many years ago, the emotional wounds associated with these scars were still tender. I have to admit, I built some walls around those wounds, making it impossible for others to enter this sensitive topic. I am now grateful to God for breaking down the layers, brick by brick, to remove the walls. No longer walking my journey alone, I have been able to look back on the lies I believed and see from a new and healthy perspective.

A Note to My Younger Self

With my cleft lip and palate being my deepest insecurity, I subconsciously identified it as the source of every rejection. Each time I wasn't asked on a second or third date, I came to the same general conclusion: *He isn't interested in me because I have a cleft lip and palate.* As a dense fog hung directly in front of my face, I couldn't see even an inch beyond this falsehood. After *years* of wondering if I would ever get married, God has begun to lift the fog and help me see these feelings of rejection and being unseen more clearly. Looking back over the past ten years of dating and remaining single, I would tell my younger self one thing: Every time it didn't work out, it wasn't always about the cleft lip and palate. Could he not have been interested in me because of my cleft lip and palate? Sure, *but more than likely it wasn't the reason.* He might not have been interested for a multitude of reasons. I could have been too tall. Too short. Too talkative. Not talkative enough. Too blonde. Not blonde enough. The list goes on forever. It's exhausting to think about all the possibilities!

I must confess. I'm tired of riding the crazy train of hyper-analyzing my physical appearance. I've since resolved to save myself the exhausting mental calisthenics of trying to figure out what another person is thinking or looking for in a relationship. No longer is my primary focus whether someone notices my scars. My primary focus is to become a woman who loves the Lord with all her heart. And maybe in the process, I will find a man who loves the Lord with all of his.

While I do believe that we should ask ourselves if we are someone another person would want and be blessed to be married to, this question should be about our *godly character* instead of our physical appearance. Looking back, my primary concern should have been, "Am I a person who is developing the character that would most importantly honor God and, secondly, make a great spouse?" Am I someone who is patient, kind, long-suffering, faithful, and joyful? Or am I self-centered, quick to anger, and care more for myself than others around me?

I no longer ask God why I'm single. But my primary question, instead, is, "Am I honoring *You* in all that I do?" "Lord, am I doing what *You* have required of me?"

> And now, Israel, what does the Lord your God require of you? He requires only that you fear the Lord your God, and *live in a way that pleases him*, and *love him* and *serve him with all your heart and soul*. And you must always *obey the Lord's commands* and decrees that I am giving you today for your own good. (Deuteronomy 10:12-13)

More than I want to be chosen for marriage, I want to live in a way that pleases God. I want to love and serve Him with all my heart and obey His commands. I want to do what is right: love mercy and walk humbly with God.[1]

My last date did not go so well. At the start of the meal, the conversation was forced and laborious. With time, my nerves settled, and the conversation seemed to flow with greater ease. Just as I was starting to think there could be a second date in our future, the evening seemed to end abruptly. Honestly, I'm not sure why. Walking to my car confused, I drove home to my quiet house. Instead of binge eating a tub of ice cream, for the first time, I was at peace in the midst of rejection. I did not try to "figure out" what he didn't like about me. I didn't replay each topic of conversation, each facial expression, or my comments and responses. Instead, *I trusted the sovereignty of God.*

I told Him if He didn't open the door for marriage at this time, then I would continue to honor Him in the ways He has asked. I would continue to be faithful in helping with the youth group. I would spend time in His Word and to do my job well. I'm still waiting on marriage, but I'm not waiting on life. Life has begun; and I'm on an adventure with God, the most constant and stable being I've ever known. I cannot miss the good things that God has given me today as I wait on what He has for me tomorrow.

Waiting Well with God

Waiting. Remaining single into your thirties can make you grow weary in waiting. As junior high kids selecting dodgeball teams, it seems like everyone else is being chosen but you're still standing against the wall waiting for your name to be called.

"I want Susie."

"I'll take Tommy."

Soon you look around and see everyone on a team.

Except *you.*

Although waiting hasn't always been a fun process, I have found a great treasure in waiting. Waiting allows time for maturity. It allows time for personal growth. With God, there is always *purpose* in our waiting. When we're waiting on God, we must always remember that God is in the waiting and working on our hearts as we allow Him. Waiting with God has helped me realize the error of my thinking. Thinking back to my childhood interaction with the woman at the jewelry store, I can now see the heavy depth of my insecurity and desire for validation from a man. *Maybe,* I would get married too.

The prospect of marriage was my source of validation. In other words, if I were married, *maybe* I would believe my cleft lip and palate is not as bad as I thought. If a guy said I were beautiful, *maybe* that would make all my feelings of not being beautiful enough vanish forever. To me, if I were married, surely I was not as ugly as I believed. One of the most dangerous things we can do is look for a relationship in order to feel better about ourselves. If we allow others to validate us, then others can also invalidate us. God alone is our validation. We need no other stamp of approval than His.

In my waiting, most of my friends have married. Thankfully, they do not hide the struggles of married life. Seeing their joys and struggles has helped me keep marriage in a healthy perspective. From the front row of their lives, I have seen that while marriage is a blessing, it's not a means to achieve our own personal happiness or validation.

The marriage of a man and woman is a beautiful picture of Christ's love for His bride, the church. Marriage paints a picture of Christ and His love for us. The gift of marriage is a picture of His passion and His sacrificial love for His people.[2] Marriage is an opportunity for partnership, companionship, spiritual intimacy, demonstrating the sacrificial love of Jesus Christ, and pursuing God together. In having time to gain an understanding of the true purpose of marriage, I'm thankful for waiting. God has been gracious to me. He has helped me consider a variety of people in my life who have married and others who remain single. I have seen women of all different colors, shapes, and sizes walk down the aisle and marry men of all different colors, shapes, and sizes. I have seen women and men with cleft lip and palates get married; and I have seen men and women with no physical abnormalities remain single.

At no point in any wedding ceremony has the bride or groom listed the shape of the other person's nose as a reason why they chose to marry one another. Not one couple has ever told me that the shape of their spouse's nose helped them have a wonderful marriage of sixty-five years. While I'm clearly joking, there is a hint of seriousness to this statement. These truths have helped me understand that the belief that I'm single or unchosen because of my cleft lip and palate simply isn't true.

With time and maturity, I have been able to see past my scars and no longer wonder if I will find someone who didn't mind the scars or the appearance of my nose. I have learned that when we surrender our lives to Christ, our physical appearance does not hinder the will of God. If God's will for my life is marriage, I know my future husband will *not* find me beautiful *in spite of* my cleft lip and palate. Instead, he will find my cleft *a part* of my beauty, as it has helped shape me into who I am.

I no longer desire validation from marriage, but I hope for marriage to enjoy a partnership with my husband and to continue our purpose, together, in Christ. I don't want to be a life-sucking validation machine, constantly looking to others to assure me of my value. My aim is to find someone who would whole-heartedly pursue God and desire to spread the Good News of Jesus alongside me. Rather than blaming my cleft lip and palate for my singleness, I now understand that I'm waiting on God's timing. Knowing that God is sovereign and withholds nothing good from us, we can trust our journey to Him.[3]

The saddest thing *is not* if we remain single the rest of our lives. Singleness isn't a disease; it's a state of being. The saddest thing is if we miss our own journey with God because we focused on wanting another person's journey instead. In Christ, there is no better journey than your own with Him; the question isn't which phase of your journey you're in, but Who is at the center of your journey. Choose to live it with Him. Whether single or married, our hearts must anchor in Him.

Healing the Wounds

In our feelings of being unchosen, overlooked, and rejected, it can seem as if no one else understands our pain. One of the greatest blessings in my life is having three siblings that truly care for me. Growing up, we engaged in our share of sibling squabbles. Whether it was fighting over whose turn it was to play Mario Brothers or arguing over who had more orange juice and popcorn during movie night, we were ready and willing to fight our battles. Regardless of how much we bickered amongst ourselves, there was one golden rule: *no one* picked on my brother and me because of our cleft lips and palates.

During recess, my sister and her classmate were climbing to the top of the monkey bars. With my sister's recess nearing the end, my brother's class came outside for the start of their recess time. As my brother entered the playground, her classmate leaned over, and said, "Look, here comes Flat Nose." With a small flame of fire igniting within her, my sister turned to him and demanded, "Take it back!" Unapologetically, he slyly questioned, "What are you, a flat nose lover?" With the flame nearly bursting inside of her, she offered one more chance for repentance. Making the same demand but this time with an added warning, she retorted "Take it back.....or else!"

Disregarding the final warning, laughing, he pointed towards my brother and yelled, "Flaaatnooossseee!" In T-minus one second, my sister transformed from a little school girl playing on the monkey bars into Xenia Warrior Princess. Gathering all the force she had, she quickly shoved him off the monkey bars. Jumping down near him, she kicked him one time for added measure.

My sister took a trip to the principal's office, but she had my brother's back. She understood his pain and did what she could to protect him. In my own journey, through their actions, my siblings taught me that they cared for me as well. They knew my pain. They saw my rejection.

While it encouraged my heart to know my siblings saw my rejection and cared, the truth that my Heavenly Father understands my rejection moves my heart in an immeasurable way. Jesus doesn't know about my rejection in a mere intellectual way. He doesn't just know I feel rejected. He knows of my rejection because He has experienced rejection firsthand.

Jesus, being fully human and fully God, identifies with our human condition. During His time on earth, Jesus was tempted, hungry, called names, mocked, and laughed at.[4] Jesus experienced a multitude of human emotions, including rejection. After performing miracles among the people, they begged Him to go away and leave them alone.[5] When He spoke, the crowds became furious, mobbed Him, and intended to push Him off a cliff.[6] He was despised and rejected and knew the deepest grief.[7] Jesus offered Himself as Savior and *still* some rejected Him. Outsiders weren't the only ones to reject Jesus; some who were closest to His inner circle rejected Him as well. His own disciple, Judas, dined with Jesus and ate of His food yet turned his back on Him. Jesus was not emotionless when He suffered betrayal of a close disciple; it was a source of profound grief.[8]

Jesus is our high priest who sympathizes with our weakness.[9] He himself has gone through suffering so He could help us when we suffer.[10] Not only does He sympathize with our weaknesses but at this very moment He sits at the right hand of the Father making intercession for us.[11] I remember when I realized that Jesus was compassionate, sympathizing with my pain, and interceding on my behalf. It touched my heart. When I prayed, I envisioned Jesus, full of compassion and understanding, praying on my behalf, knowing exactly what I was feeling. Prayer became like talking to a friend who shared the same struggles. I was talking to *Jesus*, my Comforter and the One who is intimately present in my deepest pain of rejection.

There are seasons in our lives when we feel unchosen and we wonder if anyone will ever choose us. During these times, we must anchor our hearts on the truth that God always chooses us. From the very beginning, God always has and *always will* choose us as His own.

Becoming Tender and Responsive

In our moments of rejection, God is *so* close and near, ready to bandage the wounds of our heart that we suffer in this battle called life. Although God can and will provide care and healing, we must allow Him to work within us. Attempting to heal our own wounds, we become self-protecting or aggressive in our striving to avoid rejection at all costs.

The self-protecting individual hides from others and situations that may provoke future wounds. She decides in her heart that the pain of losing or being rejected in relationships is too much to bear. By a means to protect her heart, she builds a wall and hides behind it. Offering her heart to no one, she never trusts or is vulnerable again. She isolates herself. She backs away from those around her, fearing they may bring another wound. Possibly a deeper wound than the last. She vows in her heart that no one will ever hurt her again as she refuses to offer anything to anyone, not even the smallest remaining pieces of her heart.

Another woman tries to heal the wound on her own by becoming aggressive. She says, "No one will hurt me again, and I will be sure of it." This woman is angry, bitter, and brash. She is confrontational, continually seeking and calling out the errors of others. She rehearses every wrong committed against her, some of the wrongs are real and others a figment of her imagination. She falsely believes that everyone is out to get her.

Like the self-protecting woman, she too offers her heart to no one and never becomes vulnerable with anyone. But she does not hide from others. Instead, she drives them away with her accusations and bitterness. She makes sure to ruin all her relationships so there will be no one left close enough to hurt to her. She promises that no one will ever hurt her again. In her anger and resentment, she makes that happen as she plows a destructive trail that sends others running far from her.

Maybe you relate to the self-protecting woman or the aggressive woman. I know I've created my own barriers throughout the years. But we must keep God at our center; with our tender and loving God in our midst, we can unharden our hearts and take down the barriers we've created. In our moments of rejection, we must not shut down our hearts and become cold and resentful. We must ask the Great Healer to heal our wounds and keep our hearts alive as we rest in His love and acceptance. As God's holy people, we must clothe ourselves with tenderhearted mercy, kindness, humility, and gentleness.

Being tenderhearted does not mean that we have no fight within us. As a former athlete, I struggled with the concept of being tenderhearted. While competing against an intense rivalry, I couldn't be tenderhearted towards my opponent. In the midst of intense competition, grit, determination, and fight are required to have any hope of victory. In life's dealings, evil can push on our doorstep, and we must be willing to engage the fight. Digging both heels firmly into the ground, we become unrelenting in our pursuit of victory.

When I speak of the cultivation of a tender heart, I'm talking about the condition of the heart after fighting the battle. After the battle, we must let our hearts recover from the siege. A tender heart moves to love. A tender heart moves toward compassion. A tender heart can *feel*. A heart that has been through the wringer of this life and left untouched by the love of the Father is callused and numb. A tender heart isn't naïve or oblivious to the wounds of rejection she has received from the assault of living this life. A tender heart is someone who, after battling rejection, lays at the feet of Jesus and asks Him to bring life and restoration to her heart.

The Father comes and softens our hearts. He gives us one more reason to hope, one more reason to *expect*, and one more reason to trust in Him. As we melt in the Father's arms, coming undone before him, we lay our swords down, surrendering and resting in Him. We ask Him to allow us to feel once again. We ask that He make our hearts *tender* and *responsive* once again.

CHAPTER 6

Finding True Strength

"God's strength in your weakness is His presence in your life."

- Andy Stanley

"Tears are prayers too. They travel to God when we can't speak."

– Author Unknown

It takes strength to endure physical pain in this world. The repair of a cleft lip and palate isn't a gentle process. At approximately fourteen years of age, the doctor removed cartilage from my rib and placed it in my nose to add height and dimension so it was not so flat in appearance. To prevent the cartilage from moving while it healed, he placed a screw at the top of my nose, right between my eyes.

This surgery was quite invasive. There was much swelling. After arriving home, the area around my eyes continued to swell. Within the next 24 hours, they swelled completely shut. I was unable to see. It was not all a bad experience as my gracious siblings waited on me hand and foot. The next day the swelling began to go down, and I could barely open my eyes to see where I was walking.

As far back as I can remember, I always felt the need to be tough during my procedures. I felt the need to bounce back quickly after surgery, often pushing past physical recovery recommendations. One summer when I was in middle school, my parents began remodeling our house. Before my dad left for work, he tasked my brothers with small projects. From shingling the porch roof, moving stone to the foundation, or tearing out old drywall, they had plenty of tasks to keep them busy. This summer in particular, my brothers were putting particleboard around the house to prepare for siding. Sitting inside healing from my surgery, I could hear the pounding of nails outside. Feeling confined and growing restless inside the house, I convinced myself I could and should help my brother. Walking outside, I found him high on a ladder. With the fresh gauze still across my face, I told him, "I can help."

Placing my own hammer and nails into my tool belt, I climbed a shorter ladder to assist him with the job. After a few minutes of pounding nails, I turned to my right and saw my grandma standing there with a look of dismay. She came to visit me as I recovered and was dumbfounded to find me on a ladder working in the summer heat. She, of course, told me to get down.

It was my mentality. I believed I could push through *anything*. After one procedure, eagerly wanting to go home, I told the doctor and nurses that I felt great so they would release me. Approximately twenty minutes into the car ride home, I began puking in the car my parents purchased six months prior! Not only did I feel the need to be physically tough, I also felt the need to be emotionally tough. In the midst of a struggle, I didn't give myself permission to cry. Instead, I held my emotions within, always trying to appear outwardly as if all was well. While surgeries require a level of physical toughness, I found great danger in my mentality to push through every challenge.

If we are always trying to be "tough," there is great threat that our outward "toughness" will toughen our hearts as well. When we feel the need to be tough, we say things like, "I always have to be strong" or, "I take care of others but no one takes care of me." We quickly find ourselves being the shoulder that others cry on, yet never being raw with our own emotions and taking the time to cry our own tears. If we find ourselves consistently in warrior mode, believing we have to do it all and never with child-like faith, it'll do us well to rest in the arms of God and operate in His strength rather than our own.

Holding Back the Tears

One of my earliest memories of holding back tears was when I was in the fourth grade. Dealing with continual ear infections, my mom took me to an Ear Nose and Throat Doctor (ENT). Leaning me back in the chair, the doctor completed a *very* brief exam. Turning away from me, he turned towards my mom. He informed her I needed surgery to repair a hole in my eardrum so I could hear better. He explained the steps of the procedure in a matter-of-fact way, which was no comfort to me.

I held it together in the office. I fought so hard to keep tears from welling up. Shutting the car door, my leaking tears flooded like the breaking of a dam. I was overwhelmed with the proposal of another operation. For my fourth-grade heart; it was too much.

Frustrated with the inability to hear well, I did want to hear better; but I didn't want another surgery. I told my mom I didn't want to go back. Could we try another doctor? Could we get a second opinion? After all, I could hear well enough to get by. We did get a second opinion. To my delight, my parents and doctor decided to wait and not repair the hole.

Fast forward to my college years. Waking up with the sensation of a cotton ball stuck in my left ear, sound fell flat. The normal vibrancy of sound felt dead and hallow. I labored to hear. Much more than my usual effort. Now I could barely hear out of that ear.

Another visit to the ENT confirmed that my eardrum had torn. Surgery was required to repair. Frustrated, yet wanting to hear again, this time, I knew I had to proceed.

The first night of recovery was rough. I laid in the living room recliner in the silence of the night. Dark was all around me, but my eyes were wide open. I couldn't sleep. Although the night gave no sound, I heard a beating in my ear. It sounded like a heartbeat.

Ba-boom. Ba-boom. Ba-boom. Ba-boom. Ba-boom. Ba-boom. Steady and constant.

Ba-boom. Ba-boom. Ba-boom. Ba-boom. Ba-boom. Ba-boom. The noise continued throughout that long night.

Tossing and turning.

Upset and Frustrated.

I just wanted to sleep.

I wanted to cry.

Something within me felt like I shouldn't. I felt the need to push through. Overwhelmed. Frustrated. Completely done. Yet, I was *not* going to be weak. I was *not* going to cry.

Finding Strength through Tears

I held the tears back many other times. Most of the time, I was successful. A few times, regardless how hard I tried, I couldn't stop them from bursting forth. One day at school, a kid was making fun of my cleft lip and palate; and no matter how hard I fought, I was unable to hold it together. Immediately when I got home, my mom asked me how my day went. Tears started pouring down my face.

Embracing me with a hug, my mom and I sat together on the couch. After what seemed like an eternity of tears, I continued to cry more intensely. I still hadn't told her what went wrong; I couldn't even get the words out of my mouth. Knowing I couldn't speak, I waited for my mom's comforting words. I waited and waited, but she said nothing.

Finally looking up at my mom, her eyes were puffy red as she wiped the tears falling from her cheeks. Too busy with my own tears, I hadn't noticed that tears had been streaming down her face. Unable to speak herself, she continued to embrace me with a hug.

She never did say anything.

She didn't have to.

She taught me with her tears.

When life's circumstances were overwhelming, my mom taught me one of the most valuable lessons: *when life hurts, it's okay to cry.* I don't always have to be tough and hide my pain. It's healthy to cry. Instead of suppressing within, I'm learning to cry tears *well*. In this, I'm healing well.

I learned another lesson that day. When others are hurting, we don't always need to have words to heal the pain. My mom had no words that day. Yet her presence and tears brought healing to my heart. She did not try to rush me through my pain. No. She grieved *with* me.

Although she was a great example for me, if I'm honest, allowing others to grieve effectively is still a challenge for me. Most often, I'm low key on the emotion scale. I ride the emotion waves steady, never getting too high or too low. On the rare occasions I am tearful, I still tend to hide them more than I like to admit. Although I'm growing, I'm still not particularly comfortable with others expressing their emotions. In fact, I diligently keep anyone who is expressing his or her emotions at least a few healthy arm's distances away. In the event that he or she would want a hug, I wouldn't be the first option. I give the best "side hugs" of anyone I know. I'm seldom the first one to offer a hug as a greeting or goodbye. Even my good friend calls me out for my "hugging style." She doesn't approve of my method. When hugging, I do so quickly and give a little pat on the back as if I'm saying, *Tough loss champ, but don't give up* to the junior high boy who lost his pony league baseball game.

I think many can relate to the challenge of comforting someone who is hurting and expressing emotion, unsure of what to say or do.

My tendency is to offer words to try to "fix" the problem. When someone loses a loved one, I resort to words like, "Well they're in a better place." If a friend loses her job, my response is, "It's all good. God's got something better." If someone confided to me that God seems distant, I respond with, "That's just a feeling; you know God is always with you. The Bible says so." In other words, it's a passive aggressive *"Suck it up, buttercup," and get over it; you're making me uncomfortable with your feelings* response. Although the words I speak may be truth (i.e. God does have all things under control), I'm learning to allow others to grieve and not just push them along with encouraging words. Many times, I wish I could wave my magic wand and "make it all better," but I cannot. In these times, I'm learning the simple act of praying with, listening to, or offering a hug or a shoulder to cry on to a friend in the midst of heartache. To heal, we must mourn well *together*.

It's Okay to Cry

It's okay to cry. After all, even Jesus wept. Throughout His time on earth, Jesus shed tears of personal suffering[1] and tears of compassion.[2] At His friend's grave, He was deeply grieved.[3] Jesus did more than cry a few tears; Jesus *lamented*.

Lamenting is passionately expressing grief. It's expressing unhappiness about something or a situation. Lamenting is to mourn aloud, wail, or to express great sorrow.[4] Jesus lamented when He felt abandoned on the cross. He cried, "My God, my God, why have you abandoned me?"[5]

Knowing Jesus lamented, we gain incredible insight to the heart of God. We can be sure that He is not indifferent to our grief. God promises to provide comfort. He tracks all of our sorrows. Not a tear goes unnoticed. He collects them in a bottle and records each one in His book.[6] He saves those who are crushed in spirit.[7] In Christ, though tears may last through the night, joy comes in the morning.[8]

Jesus invites all who are weary and heavy burdened to come to Him, and He will give us rest.[9]

Tears are a result of our living in a fallen world. Tears are a result of things not being as God intended in the Garden of Eden. Tears are not a weakness. Tears are certainly not a lack of faith in God. All throughout Scripture, God's beloved shed tears. Moses cried. Abraham cried. David frequently poured his heart out to God, telling Him of his fears, concerns, and sorrows. David did not put on a happy "fake it till you make it" face. Rather, he poured out his grief before God.

Real and raw.

He poured it out.

Our tears are an invitation to fellowship with God. The One who is near the brokenhearted calls us to weep with those who are weeping. In our tears, we can draw near to God in our distress and allow our hearts to be enlarged through suffering. In the midst of the pain, when we turn our eyes to the promise of God, we see that He will restore us and wipe every tear from our eyes.[10]

Crying is the overflow of grief and ache in our hearts. Rather than suppress it, you and I should let the grief overflow. Knowing that Jesus lamented and that almost half the Psalms are laments,[11] I'm encouraged that we too, can and should lament in the mist of tragedy or heartache.

In his book, *God Behaving Badly*, David Lamb describes the basic pattern of a lament in the psalms. The five steps of the pattern include: Invocation, Complaint, Petition, Trust, and Praise. To understand better, David outlines the steps in relation to Psalm 13.

Invocation: *Oh Lord,*

Complaint: *How long will you forget me? Forever? How long will you look the other way? How long must I struggle with anguish in my soul, with sorrow in my* *heart every day? How long will my enemy have the upper hand?*

Petition: *Turn and answer me, O Lord My God! Restore the sparkle to my eyes or I will die. Don't let my enemies gloat saying, "We have defeated him!" Don't let them rejoice at my downfall.*

Trust: *But I will trust in your unfailing love. I will rejoice because you have rescued me.*

Praise: *I will sing to the Lord because He is good to me.*[12]

If we lament in accordance to the layout of the Psalms, the last two steps include a drawing back into *trust* and *praise.* If we only complain before God, we enter a place of deep anguish and sorrow that is difficult to escape. If we focus on our complaint more than on the trust and praise of God, we could find ourselves hopeless.

Just as our earthly parents will not let us stay on their laps and cry forever, God also wants to move us forward by picking us up and strengthening us once again. The brilliant God we serve knew complaining alone would be a pattern in our lives if it were our focus. Therefore, He includes the last two steps to keep us out of the pit of despair and return us to our faith in Him and His goodness.

While there is a time to mourn, there is also a season to rejoice.[13] To heal, we must also allow God to strengthen our hearts and move us forward past the pain. King David cried out to God in his distress yet understood that God heard his prayer and would answer him by giving him strength.[14] In Christ, we do not stay in our grief forever. Although life may knock us into times of intense pain, we cannot remain in the grief.

When life is hard, thanksgiving and praise are truly a sacrifice and extremely difficult to initiate. There may be times when we're so broken that all we can express is a mumbled or weak, "God you're good." In these moments, whatever we can muster up, our praise turns us back to Him. After we muster up a little, we try a little more and a little more. Soon we're overflowing with praise. Regardless of my feelings, the truth of God's faithfulness stands and isn't subject to my situation. Praise and thanksgiving bring me back to a place of trust in God's character and promises despite how I may feel in the moment.

Releasing our tears before the Lord, we find strength. Our weak and feeble knees are strengthened when we realize He can handle everything we cannot. We joyfully praise Him knowing that while we cannot carry every burden on our own, He can. In our tears and frustration, we realize we don't have all the answers and that we're powerless without Him. We stand in fortitude when we become less and He becomes our all.

Through all the tears and heartache, we must anchor our hearts on this one truth: *in all His ways, God is good*. He has no equal and His wonderful deeds and plans for us are too numerus to list.[15] When we hurt, there is no place to run except into the loving arms of Jesus. In all of our struggles, frustration and confusion, we hold tight to what is good; *we hold tight to Jesus.*

True Strength: Knowing I am Never Forsaken

We find true strength when we understand that God never leaves us nor forsakes us.[16] Sometimes God seems incredibly near. Other times, He feels distant and unreachable—as if my prayers are bouncing off the floor of heaven, like a letter returned to sender, never arriving at the desired address.

During my first two years of college, nothing was going the way I hoped. My family and friends were hundreds of miles away; and God felt a million miles away. After tearing my ACL and prematurely ending my high school basketball career, I desperately wanted to have a successful college basketball career. What I thought was going to be a new beginning and redemption of my high school career was one failure after another. I struggled to play consistently well. I desired more playing time and to have a significant role within the team. It just was not happening.

One afternoon, frustrated with my failures on the basketball court, I angrily questioned, "God, do you even care?" My frustration with God had been cumulating. In selfishness, I didn't understand why He didn't make my basketball career turn out the way *I wanted*. I was working hard in practice and still wasn't good enough.

I had no desire to go to church, but I reluctantly attended knowing I couldn't give up on God. At a Sunday service, the praise and worship team sang the song "Forever" by Chris Tomlin. The chorus sings: "Forever God is faithful; forever God is strong. Forever God is with us; forever." The refrain repeats, *"His love endures forever."*

I wasn't feeling the words. I wasn't feeling *anything*. The words were hard to believe because God felt so distant. He didn't seem to be forever faithful. He didn't even seem to hear my prayers or care about my basketball career.

After leaving church that Sunday, "Forever" played on the radio a few times that week. Each time the song played, it caught my attention and the words began to replay in my mind. Beginning to enjoy the song, I downloaded it to my MP3 player and repeated it many times throughout the week.

The upcoming weekend, my extended family gathered to celebrate my grandpa's 80th birthday. Missing my family and needing a break from school and basketball, I was excited to go home for even a short time. With a 3.5-hour drive home, I had plenty of time to listen to music and Chris Tomlin's song "Forever" made the song list on the drive home. After a restful weekend with my family, I packed my car up, feeling refreshed for the journey back to school. As I was saying goodbye to my mom, she began to cry. She told me she didn't want me to leave. Blowing her off, I told her there was nothing to worry about and I had to go back to school. Later, I found out she felt very uneasy and prayed for me as I drove back.

Preparing for my road trip, I tuned into the clearest radio station in the area. A few minutes into the trip, the song I was playing all week, Chris Tomlin's song "Forever," began playing on the local radio station. It was as if the song were constantly following me. I was forced to consider: maybe God did care. *Maybe* He was faithful. *Maybe* He did see me.

While on US 23 near Ann Arbor, Michigan, a light rain began to fall. With my cruise control set to over 70 MPH, I headed into a curve. Suddenly, my tire hit a pothole and I began hydroplaning, spinning out of control. Shutting my eyes before the impact, my car turned sideways and T-boned into a guardrail, pulling six poles out of the ground. Opening my eyes, I saw a white powdery substance coming from the airbag.

With adrenaline rushing, I swung open my door and exited the car. Seeing my belongings that flew through my shattered back window, I jumped over a small ditch to retrieve them. Witnesses of the accident quickly cautioned me to stop, fearing I may be injured. Honoring their instructions, I sat down. Within a few minutes, the ambulance arrived. At the hospital, the nurses and doctors assessed me and with time, they cleared me. I hadn't sustained any injuries.

Within a few hours, my parents arrived at the hospital and we ventured to collect my belongings and license plates from the tow truck company. The woman at the front desk had become aware of the extensive damage to my car. She was amazed I hadn't sustained any injuries. She pointed us towards my car, seeing it for the first time since the accident. The damage was extensive. The passenger side pushed inward, stopping at the middle console, leaving the driver's and left back passenger seats the only intact portion of the car.

Looking the vehicle over, my mom noticed something behind the shattered windshield. On the dashboard lie my open Bible covered in tiny pieces of glass. Although my laundry bag and book bag flew out my back window, my Bible landed open on the dashboard. Picking it up, the employee shut it and held it out for me to take. "Wait!"

my mom exclaimed, "What page was that opened to?" Finding the pieces of glass now serving as a bookmark, he reopened the Bible to Psalm 136. It read:

"Give thanks to the Lord, for he is good! *His faithful love endures forever.*"

This was the most miraculous event I ever witnessed. Not only was it a miracle that I walked away without injury, but God clearly spoke to me in that moment as well. Even when I do not feel His presence or when things do not go as I hope, He is involved in every detail of my life. He will never abandon me. He will never forsake me. Just as the song was teaching me throughout the week, our God is faithful; and his love endures forever!

This truth changed my life. I wish I could say that I never again doubted God's abiding presence in my life. I still do at times. Some days it's easier to be led by how I feel for the day rather than the truth that God will never leave me nor forsake me. This Christmas my parents gifted me a shadow box to remember the car accident and God's hand through it all. Reflecting on the event, God's abiding faithfulness and enduring love come back to the forefront of my walk with Him. Strength arises as I remember and contemplate the goodness and faithfulness of God in my life.

As I turn back to the 136th chapter of the Psalm, I cannot miss the repetition of the phrase: *His faithful love endures forever.* I cannot help but wonder that maybe in His faithful love, God repeated this truth twenty-six times because He *knew* I needed the reminder. He is gentle. He is kind. He loves us with an enduring love. He is faithful. He builds us up and encourages our hearts. He promises *never to* leave nor forsake us, no matter how we may feel.

True Strength: Being Authentic

A college classmate and future Speech-Language Pathologist, Stephanie, was also born with a cleft lip and palate. She was a great encouragement to me, each semester confidently sharing her personal journey with one of our classes. After meeting her in the class and learning about my experience, she invited me to share my story alongside her.

The mere thought of standing in front of thirty students, openly sharing my challenges, made me grow uneasy. The feelings of inadequacy, vulnerability, and fear of rejection that I worked hard to suppress began to resurface. I told her I needed time to think about it; being authentic was terrifying. Being authentic turned my stomach in knots. My heart felt as if it were about to jump out of my chest. It felt like the walls I built around me were threatened, and the false security I had created felt like it was going to collapse if pressed too hard. I feared what others would think; would they think less of me? Could they even relate to my experience?

After considering a long time, I finally built up the courage and reluctantly accepted Stephanie's invitation to share my personal journey. Looking back, I'm grateful she encouraged me to share our stories *together*. I realized I wasn't alone, and I never regretted the decision. After all, I wasn't the first person in the world to have a cleft lip and palate, and I wouldn't be the last.

Sharing my story helped me realize that, although not all stories are the same, we can still learn from others' experiences. Not everyone will relate to my entire story. However, they may glean a piece. When we lay out our whole deck of cards through authenticity, we allow the listener the freedom to pick up what they choose. Really, they don't have to understand it all. Who knows—later, they may comprehend more.

I realized through the experience that strength is not denying that something has hurt us. In my ignorance, I thought that if I didn't talk about the challenge of being born with a cleft lip and palate that I'd somehow be protected from further hurt. Instead, hiding my experiences only deepened the feelings of being alone and insecure. Denying my struggles kept me locked up and bound to them. But being real invites those who are struggling to take refuge.

When we choose to be authentic, we support others by reminding them that *they are not alone in their struggles.*

True Strength: Allowing God to Go Deeper than the Scars

I have since found strength in not hiding my struggle from others. And I have found even greater strength in not trying to hide my struggle from God. Really, I cannot hide even my inmost thoughts or concerns from Him anyway. He knows all things. Living authentic before the Lord meant that I needed to stop putting up walls and acting like all was well. Little by little, I opened up to God, asking Him to heal my whole heart, only as He could.

At the end of each college basketball practice, we shot ten free throws—one of the most important shots that could cost us (or award us) the game. It was so important to learn to be mentally prepared to score our shots even when we were physically exhausted. Once each team member completed her shots, we would all line up on the baseline and run sprints for each missed attempt. Being a below-average free-throw shooter, I spent a lot of quality time running sprints. I ran so much that the thought of practice alone made me want to vomit. I worried how stupid I looked missing my shots. I questioned whether I deserved to be on the team if I weren't mentally strong enough to make the shots that mattered most. With my nerves on the fritz, I became progressively worse at shooting free throws.

During one summer break, my friend Erica and I routinely practiced shooting free throws at a local high school gymnasium. I was shooting carefree and relaxed, making most of my attempts. Admitting this performance was not my usual, I confided in her how scared and nervous I became while shooting free throws during practice. She asked, "Stacey, what are you afraid of?" Without hesitation, I irritably replied, "Haven't you been listening to me? I'm afraid of missing my free throws!"

As a smirk widened across her face, she replied, "You are not afraid of missing free throws, *you're afraid to fail*. This isn't at all about free throws. This is about your fear of failure and your fear of what other people think of you. If you don't let God deal with *that issue*, in two years when basketball is finished, you'll just transfer the fear of failure onto something different." Although I hated to admit it, Erica was right. The fear of failure permeated my life. As she warned, upon graduation, the fear of failure didn't relent.

With great insight from my friend, I'm learning to see past the superficial and ask God to deal with the dire issues within my heart. I found freedom by no longer hiding my issues but rather letting God get to the root of my struggles. Finally giving Him the reigns, I asked that He take away my insecurities and heal my heart. Nevertheless, He didn't stop at my insecurities; *He wanted my whole heart and every aspect of my life.*

God strengthened me by revealing what my struggle really was.
I thought it was about missing free throws.
It was really about my fear of failure.
I thought it was about the scars on my lip.
It was really that I focused more on my own scars than Christ's scars.
It wasn't about the names I was called.
It was that I gave the words of man more attention and value than the Word of God.
It wasn't about believing I was ugly.
It was about my false belief that God makes ugly things.

He did not do a mere superficial work and allow me to keep my cleft lip and palate as my false identity. He taught me that I didn't need a higher and more positive view of myself; rather, I needed a *higher* view of Him. He did not want me hiding nor magnifying my own struggles; but I needed to *magnify* Jesus Christ. Making Him the Lord of my life, I can trust all things to the One who holds my life in His hands. No longer focusing and fussing over my cleft; I focus on and make *much* of Him.

CHAPTER 7

Fearfully and Wonderfully Made

"How cool is it that the same God, who created mountains, and oceans, and galaxies, looked at you and thought the world needed one of you too?"

- Author Unknown

"I would rather be what God chose to make me than the most glorious creature that I could think of, for to have been born in God's thought, and then made by God, is the dearest, grandest, and most precious thing in thinking."

- C.S. Lewis

"Say cheese!" the woman behind the camera instructed. She really didn't need to tell me; I was already smiling ear-to-ear, ensuring to show off the tooth that I pulled out the day prior. I was proud of my missing tooth. It was a stamp in my passport of life; a signal I was growing up. Missing baby teeth serve as a badge of honor for many kids. I remember my brother walking tall and proud when he lost one of his teeth, excited to tell anyone who would listen about his rite of passage. Pointing to the gum line that once held his baby tooth secure, he eagerly filled the listener in on how he successfully removed it:

"I tied one end of the string to my tooth and the other side to the door knob. Then my brother slammed the door shut, and it came out!"

All the boys in the group were impressed.

Missing teeth.

In our childhood, they earn us money from the tooth fairy.

In our childhood, grins with random missing teeth are cute.

I lost many baby teeth. However, where the cleft formed, there were never baby teeth to lose. While some only want their two front teeth for Christmas, as a teenager, I had my two front teeth; all I wanted was my lateral incisors and canines. Wish as I may, lacking adequate bone support, the teeth never came. By the sixth grade, my classmates' scattered teeth all filled in with their adult teeth. It was no longer socially acceptable to have missing teeth.

Still with a few missing teeth in middle school, well, I was *embarrassed.*

The doctor told me it was time I wear a retainer with fake teeth. Being in my fragile teenage years, I was never more grateful. It surely was not comfortable, but it did its job to fill in the missing gaps so I could smile with confidence.

When out in public, I wore the cumbersome retainer, because it was more aesthetically appealing than my unfilled pre-teen smile. But when at home with my family, I seldom wore it. It was just more comfortable to be without it. And to be honest, I had *fun* with my missing teeth while in private. Removing my fake teeth, my two front teeth stood alone. Protruding my front teeth over my bottom lip, I grabbed a carrot; and in my best Bugs Bunny voice I mimicked, "What's up Doc?" While I could have fun with it at home, my missing teeth were a great source of insecurity elsewhere.

Although most are insecure in junior high, my fake teeth heightened my sensitivity. After switching orthodontists, one of my fake teeth broke, and I needed a replacement. After having dental impressions, I was fitted with my new retainer. Placing it inside my mouth and smiling into the mirror, I was mortified as they were the size of baby teeth. They were much too small! They hardly filled the gaps of my missing teeth. Whether it truly looked that bad, or if I was being a mellow dramatic teenager, I can't be sure. Nonetheless, I petitioned my mom to take me somewhere else to get a better retainer made. I begged her. There was no way I could go to school the next day looking like this! All my classmates would find out my teeth were fake!

Removing my fake teeth when I slept, sleepovers with friends were not enjoyable. While most teens would find it awesome to share a hotel room with their best friend, I dreaded my vacation to Florida. As the vacation came nearer, all I could think about was *how* I would remove my fake teeth and *where* I would keep them so my friend wouldn't find out. The plan consumed me. I tortured myself over what would be the best hiding place. I finally decided that I would wear pants with pockets to bed so I could have my retainer in my possession at all times.

I carefully waited until everyone was in bed before I took my retainer out of my mouth. I didn't want anyone trying to talk to me without my teeth. I was self-conscious because I couldn't speak as clearly as air escaped through the gaps in my natural teeth. My friend never did find out about my missing teeth that week. I accomplished the mission, but I didn't enjoy the week. My mind was only on one thing: hiding my retainer. So, after seven days, I was emotionally drained rather than on a vacation high like everyone else.

Although it was not funny in the moment, one of my favorite stories occurred one night after my ACL surgery. During the winter months, it was common for my friends and me to spend most Friday and Saturday nights at high school basketball games. This evening, my friends went to the boys' basketball game as usual. However, I couldn't join them, as I was recovering from my surgery.

I sat in the recliner with my leg in a brace and covered with an ice pack for the swelling. My brothers were on the living room floor watching television. I drifted in and out of sleep as a headlight peered through the living room window. Slowly rising from the floor to see what was going on, my brother pulled back the curtain to get a clear view. He squinted to see in the distance, then turned to me and said, "Stacey, I think your friends are here." Still dazing in and out of sleep, I hadn't registered what he'd just said. Becoming a little louder, he repeated, "Stacey, I think your friends are here."

Suddenly I shot straight up. Without any other thought, I screamed, "I don't have my retainer! Get my teeth!" As if they were two world-class athletes competing in the 100-meter dash, my brothers sprinted across the house into the bathroom where I had left my retainer for the night. Like an athlete raising his championship trophy, my brother returned with my retainer in his bare hand! We heard my friends' first knock on the door. They had stopped in to hang out on their way home from the basketball game that evening.

Obviously, I granted my brothers the Best Brothers of the Year Award for getting me out of what could have been a mortifying situation. After my nerves calmed and I had a moment to process what just happened, I couldn't help but think, "Wow, that's disgusting! He was holding my retainer in his *bare* hand! Why didn't he carry it in the container? Does he know I put that in my mouth?"

While it's fun to laugh about this story today, the insecurity of my missing teeth raised a question in my mind: How can I be fearfully and wonderfully made if I don't have all of my teeth? I mean, if God knit me together in my mother's womb, why did he forget my teeth? If I was fearfully and wonderfully made and was woven together by the Master Artist in my mother's womb, why the cleft? If the God of the Universe was so intricately involved in my formation, then why didn't He just complete the formation of my lip and palate in the womb? Did He grow weary on the job? Did He rush through the details? Did He overlook something?

Psalm 139

With the question of my formation fresh in my mind, I graduated from high school that spring and left for college in early summer. I moved to Michigan with the anticipation of a new beginning.

A fresh start.

In my eager anticipation, I failed to realize that I was not just taking my personal belongings with me. The questions and issues of my heart would also be making the trip across the Ohio-Michigan border. The question of my formation perpetuated at the forefront of my mind. Now living hundreds of miles from my family and friends, I spent many lonely evenings in my dorm room. One evening, sitting before God and reading His Word, I unknowingly embarked on a journey that would forever change my life.

Tearing my ACL just 6 months prior, with my false identities now removed, I was finally able to *receive* the truth of my formation in my mother's womb. During one of the loneliest and challenging seasons of my life, God began to unravel the lie that plagued my heart for so many years. He was teaching me to release the lie that I was ugly. He was going to show me I was no accident. He was going to show me I truly was fearfully and wonderfully made.

In the quietness of my college dorm room, I spent one of the most fruitful seasons of my life, pouring over Psalm 139. With the Bible opened in my lap and my feet propped upon my desk, I casually read the words aloud. Night after night, I meditated on this passage. Each time I read, the Holy Spirit began revealing to me the truth of my formation in my mother's womb. Soon, the reading was no longer casual, but the words began to leap off the page and penetrated my heart. I felt so alive. God was speaking to me through Scripture:

> You have searched me, Lord, and you *know* me. You know when I sit and when I rise; you perceive my thoughts from afar. You discern my going out and

my lying down; you are familiar with all my ways.
(Psalm 139:1-3 NIV)

Wow. Lord, you *know* me. You know every detail of my life. From beginning to end. Even though I'm alone in this room, I certainly am not alone. You're here.

> For you created my inmost being; you knit me together in my mother's womb. I praise you because I am fearfully and wonderfully made; your works are wonderful, I know that full well. (Psalm 139:13-14 NIV)

Lord! You were there the whole time! You created me with your very hands! *All* of your works are wonderful, including *me*!

> My frame was not hidden from you when I was made in the secret place, when I was woven together in the depths of the earth. Your eyes saw my unformed body; all the days ordained for me were written in your book before one of them came to be. (Psalm 139:15-16 NIV)

Sheesh! I was wrong. You saw every detail of my formation and did not miss one step along the way. You planned for my existence *before* I was even born. You have ordained each day that I live and every breath I breathe!

I did not immediately feel like I was fearfully and wonderfully made the first time I read Psalm 139. As I continued to focus on Psalm 139, though, the truth embedded within me and began to speak louder than how I felt in the moment. Soon, the Scripture was like a megaphone within my mind and heart, *screaming* truth and drowning out the lies that I had once believed. God's Word cut me to the core and opened my eyes to see His intimate involvement in my creation. And He wants you to know of His intimate involvement in *your* creation.

Probability

God radically changed my perspective during that season of my life. It was as if a light switch was flipped and I could now see the truth that I had been blind to for so long. Yet, at times when I thought about my birth, I still questioned my formation at times.

After my parents gave birth to my oldest brother, the doctors were not sure what caused his cleft. They told my parents that the chances of having another child with a cleft was very slim. After my oldest brother, my parents had my sister and another brother who were born healthy. Then, against the odds and to my parents' surprise, I was born with a cleft lip and palate. While my parents were not given a direct percentage, I have recently learned that the actual chance of me having a cleft was only between 2-8%. Regardless, the doctors were correct; the chances were indeed slim.

Yet here I was.

Since the medical field established that the chances were slim, I couldn't help but contemplate why it happened not only once in our family, but twice? I found that while medical statistics tell us projected probability, only *God knows what will surely be.* I cannot answer why God allowed my birth defect. However, I have found rest. Although the chances of having a cleft were quite low, the odds that God knew exactly what period of time, day, and minute I would be born and what my entire genetic make-up would be was 100%.

Although my parents were surprised to have another child with a cleft (due to the low likelihood), God was by no means surprised. Whether we're born with or without a birth defect, God still oversees our formation in our mother's womb. He still holds the entire situation in His hands and promises to work it all for our good.

God oversaw my formation in the womb, and not one detail

slipped through His fingers. Not only does God know us in our mother's womb, but He chooses individuals for specific tasks even before they come into existence.[1] Just as God created Esther for such a time as this,[2] He created each of us for this time. He created David to fight Goliath, Moses to lead the Israelites, and Abraham to be the father of many nations. He created you and me, exactly the way we are, for His purpose.

God is so personally involved in our lives that He has numbered the hairs on our head.[3] He cares for all the details of our lives. Like a good shepherd, He has intimate knowledge of His sheep. He tenderly guides, personally calling us by name.[4] He's not merely hoping for just the right genetic probability to create the person He will use for His purposes. In the same way, He creates us with a plan and purpose, never leaving it to random chance.

Trusting our Formation to Him

While sitting in a conference session, learning about genetic causes of birth defects, I suddenly felt overwhelmed. The speaker was explaining the complex genetic combinations that result in a cleft lip and palate. My initial excitement to learn something new turned to mind-numbing information overload. My brain couldn't handle the breadth of knowledge. Within mere minutes, I fully surrendered to "I have no clue what this lady is talking about." I sat in the room as she shared, suddenly remembering that, even though this woman's extent of knowledge seemed almost incomprehensible, God of the Universe knew far more. She was only scratching the surface of genetics and admitted that, after years and years of research, she still had more questions than answers.

While she still had questions, God did not have any questions. He is the one who created the DNA and genetic make-up that she was still trying to comprehend. While we have limited ability to process and retain information, God has no limits. This knowledge, which easily overwhelms our human minds, never overwhelms God.

If it were up to me, I would have designed myself differently. But thinking of the complexity of our physical make-up, and only being able to comprehend the very fundamental, stops me in my tracks.

I hit my knees in awe of God.

He is God.

I surely am not.

I cannot even understand the first three minutes of a thirty-minute presentation on genetics.

Who am I to tell God how He should form me?

I was not there in the beginning when He formed the sun, moon, stars and planets. I was not there when He formed Adam and breathed life into his lungs. Or when He created Eve from Adam's rib. I was not there for thousands of years as God has given life to billions of others. Yet, by His hands, I was created for this time and was given the gift of life. Greatly admiring His marvelous works, I no longer ask, "Why did you form me this way?"

I trust my formation to Him.

We live in these earthly bodies by trusting God, knowing He loves us and gave Himself for us.[5] When we find ourselves struggling with our physical appearance, we do well to remember we can trust God in everything. We trust Him with our finances. Our children. Our careers. Our ministries. Our marriages. We can even trust Him in the way we were formed in our mothers' wombs.

You Are the Crown of God's Creation

God has continued to work on my heart to reveal how He values His creation. Five years ago, my friend Aubrie and I drove 6,000 miles across the county to see the Grand Canyon, Yosemite, and Yellowstone National Parks. We spent much time mapping out our adventure and were careful to include stops in Moab, Utah, the

Badlands, and Vail, Colorado. Before the trip, I heard others talk fondly about these landmarks. These conversations left me energized and excited to see these places with my own eyes. Little did I know, *hearing* about God's creation did not compare to *seeing it firsthand.*

Even now, recalling our time spent in God's vast creation is a treasured memory and puts joy in my heart. I recall a warm summer night, standing on a balcony overlooking the Grand Canyon, eyeing the beautiful array of colors in the evening sky as the sun drifted behind the canyon. I revered the sunset, spreading wide across the canyon, proclaiming the works of His mighty hands. I couldn't help but feel small and insignificant in comparison to the vastness and greatness of the canyon.

At Yosemite, I stood amazed at God's power and might. Dripping in sweat after hiking to the top of the waterfall, I found the trip well worth the expended energy. As a mere human, I pushed my physical limitations to get a glimpse of the gallons upon gallons of water rolling over the rock and falling thousands of feet downward toward the base. This breathtaking scene, spoken into existence with ease and precision by the Creator of the Universe, was simply amazing.

Observing the splendor of God's creation blows my mind. It renders me speechless. Nothing seems adequate to describe how I feel. However, what astounds me even more is that the amazing God who created the universe and set it into motion, calls us the crown of all creation and has placed us in charge of everything He has made. He created the world and everything in it, yet we are His prized possession.[6] All things exist because He created what He pleased. God was *pleased* to create us.[7]

The psalmist's writes:

> When I look to the night sky and see the work of your fingers- the moon and the stars you set into place- what are mere mortals that you should think about them, human beings that you should care for them? Yet you made them only a little lower

than God and crowned them with glory and honor.
(Psalm 8:3-5)

Some try to stifle the notion that they are beautiful. It feels almost arrogant to say such a thing. However, understanding the truth that we are marvelous creations is not for a good feeling or an ego trip. When we know we're beautiful, it changes how we act toward others and ourselves. Knowing who God created us to be allows us to walk with confidence and peace within our hearts.

Knowing we are beautiful, we invite others to know they are beautiful as well. A woman who knows she is beautiful honors and glorifies her Creator, the One who makes beautiful things. A woman, who knows she is beautiful, honors God by not calling herself ugly or belittling herself. By belittling ourselves or others' physical appearance, we are rejecting what God has called *very good*.[8] To say we are ugly is to say that our Creator makes ugly things. And that is *false*.

We can look at the gorgeous sunset above Lake Tahoe, the deep green grass of the valley, or the soaring eagle gliding across the snowcapped mountains and stand in awe of the God who made this beautiful scene and still chooses *us* as the crown of creation. No matter how we try, without seeing ourselves from God's perspective, we will never be content with our outward appearance. Until we see the beauty that God sees, we're chasing the wind. Lose more weight. Add more concealer. We run in circles and chase our tails, only to discover another wrinkle on our forehead. Quick! Add more age defying moisturizer! Chase the tail. But as we start to see the beauty in *all* of God's creation, we declare that we, too, are fearfully and wonderfully made. He makes *all* things well- including *you*.

The Comparison Game

The comparison game is a dangerous trap that is now more readily available than it has ever been. Comparison to others is constantly available as we spend hours scrolling through others' Facebook profiles, wishing we looked like someone else. I too have been guilty of scrolling, wishing I had this friend's hair or this friend's body type. The comparisons only deepened my insecurities. Comparison with other women leaves me feeling inadequate and overall disappointed in God's design of me.

Comparison of ourselves to others is dangerous. It will most likely only have two results: pride or envy. When we compare, we become prideful in thinking we're better than those we believe aren't as beautiful, smart, wealthy, or successful as we are. On the other hand, when we find someone who has more than we do, we become envious of what God has given them, leaving us thankless for the blessings in our own life. The truth that we're *all* fearfully and wonderfully made has helped me find freedom from the comparison game, understanding that God has made each of us unique in our own way.

To better illustrate this point, let me make an analogy. I have a friend who is super creative and artistic. You know, the friend that could give a few pointers to Chip and Joanna Gaines. Her house is very beautiful with trendy and unique decorations and paintings. The paintings have timely inspirational sayings and Bible verses on them, all while keeping with the color scheme and overall style of the room.

When you walk in each room, you cannot help but appreciate the time, energy, and passion that was poured into each painting to make the room a beautiful place. Although she has a lot of artwork, not one piece of artwork is the same, and each piece has a specific place in the room. The room is so beautiful that when you walk in, you do not gravitate to one painting or picture. Rather you stand back and say, "This *entire* room is beautiful." Working in a profession that employs a majority of women, I occasionally find myself at continuing-education courses, seated in a large room filled with women. At the last convention, there were over 300 participants from all over the world. Being in this room of women, many of differing nationalities and ages, I began to compare myself to others and wonder how I measure up. While comparing, conviction came upon my heart.

God was not comparing us, so why was I?

Like my friend's living room, when women fill a room, each one of us comes together like the paintings adorning the walls—and God declares the scene as a whole *beautiful*. God did not make a beautiful corner of the room with the most beautiful woman over here or the ugliest over there. No. He oversaw all of their creation and made each unique and beautiful in appearance, personality, and interests. And together, we are His creation. His *good* and *beautiful* creation.

Beauty is in the Eyes of God

Beauty is in the eye of the beholder.

No wait.

Beauty is in the eye of God.

He defines beauty.

Not you.

Certainly not me.

Humanity's morphing definition of "beauty" reveals that we humans are incapable of truly knowing and recognizing beauty. Throughout generations and cultures, the pendulum of man's definition of "beauty" has swung back and forth.

Far back in Ancient Egypt, the ideal woman possessed a slender figure with narrow shoulders and a high waist. In Ancient Greece, women who were plump, full-bodied, and modeled light skin were considered most beautiful. During the Han Dynasty, beauty was defined as a woman with a slim waist, pale skin, larges eyes, and small feet. More recently, the Roaring Twenties defined beauty as a woman with a flat chest, short bob hairstyle and boyish figure. Between the 1930s and 1950s, most desirable women had curves, hourglass figures, large breasts and a slim waistline. When we got to the Swinging 60s, women with a thin body with long and slim legs were deemed beautiful. During the 80s, culture celebrated women who were tall, athletic and with toned arms. In the 90s, models were extremely thin with translucent skin. Presently, beauty is most readily defined as having a flat stomach, healthy skin, and large breasts and butt.[9]

Does all that information feel like a whirlwind within your mind? Are you mentally calculating what era your body type would fit? Not to my surprise, my body type does not really fit in any of those time periods. The good news is: we don't need to be born in the time-period that matches our body type. Despite the world's ever-changing definition of what it deems beautiful, we find rest for our weary hearts and minds in the unchanging truth that we're created perfect *just as we are.* Thousands of years ago, God said His workmanship is marvelous.[10]

It has never changed.

It never will.

It amazes me how we can see the beauty in someone else, yet we have a hard time seeing it in ourselves. When seeing photographs of models from decades past and present day, it's easy to declare that these women are certainly masterpieces and marvelous creations. Nevertheless, in all my studies, I never found a verse that read, "If you're named Miss America, then *you* are God's masterpiece."

I have never found a verse that said, "If you feel like a masterpiece, then you are."

Nothing.

Absolutely nothing.

Or to speak to my own circumstances, I have never read a verse that said, "You were fearfully and wonderfully made...well, unless you were born with a cleft lip and palate."

No. God never said that.

The same Bible Miss America reads, I read. You read. The entire world reads. *It's the same message given to all of us, no matter your race, size, shape, physical ability or disability.* God gives the same message to the professional athlete who makes millions because of her physical ability and to the woman who is bound to a wheelchair and cannot walk. We are all God's workmanship. We surely are marvelous.

In order to know if someone is beautiful in the eyes of God, we do not need to know what size of dress she wears or how well her hair and makeup looks.

The only question we need to ask is, "Did God create her?"

If the answer is *Yes* (and it is!) then she is fearfully and wonderfully made.

Period.

God does not need us to tell Him how to create beautiful things. He just invites us to sit back and admire the beauty He has created. It's our choice if we will see the beauty He has created, in others *and* ourselves.

CHAPTER 8

Victory in Death and the Hope of Eternal Bodies

"He who lays up treasures on earth spends his life backing away from his treasures. To him, death is loss. He who lays up treasures in heaven looks forward to eternity; he's moving daily toward his treasures. To him, death is gain."

-Randy Alcorn

"Good morning!" The tall, strong firefighter's voice boomed as he spoke to our kindergarten class. "This week is fire prevention week, and you're here to learn how to keep you and your family safe from fires." While I'm sure the kind man said many wise words after his opening greeting, my mind couldn't move past two words: *family* and *fire*.

While most of my classmates wanted him to stop talking so we could get to the fun part of trying on the firefighter's gear and blaring the firetruck sirens around town, I was too distraught to think about anything else but those two words. While I had no reason to fear that something traumatic was going to happen, at times I would experience a paralyzing fear of disaster striking my family and me. Despite the various situations that my fears expressed themselves, at the core was the fear of death.

The gentle firefighter wanted to keep me safe and said, "Get a fire plan in place." All I heard was, "We're all going to die!" Fire prevention week wasn't the only thing that brought intense fear, though. It really didn't take much to make me go to the worst-case scenario. When my parents went on a date and left us with a babysitter, if they didn't return after 15 minutes, well, clearly, they had died in a horrible car accident! When the news broadcasted a hurricane coming to the shores of a tropical island, in my mind, that hurricane would shortly take out my house as well (even though we lived in Michigan).

As a minor, my parents had to sign all of the forms that were required before I had any surgeries. I will never forget the first operation I had after turning eighteen. Sitting with my mom and dad, the woman turned to me and said, "Well you're eighteen so you get to sign all the papers." Sounding like a programmed robot, in record-breaking speed, she rattled off all the information she was required to share. Although I hardly could keep up with her, as she neared the end, I heard her mention, "risks and complications" and something about, *even death*. Slowing down her rate of speech she said, "Okay, so please sign here." Cautiously grabbing the pen, I felt like I was in a slow-motion replay and signed on the line.

Even with my history of fearing death, her statement didn't stop me from moving forward with the surgery. But as we were heading to the operating room, my mind was now focused on those words: *even death*. What do I know about death? Nothing, really. Well, nothing other than seeing graveyards along the road or a casket at a funeral home. Maybe I feared death because I knew nothing about it.

Throughout my twenties and early thirties, I have been intentional to learn more about death and my eternal home. Contemplating death in view of my eternal salvation with Jesus Christ taught me that death is nothing to fear. I no longer fear because, by dying on the cross, Jesus Christ broke the power of death. He set free all those who have lived their lives as slaves to the fear of dying.[1] He stands tall, holding the keys to the grave so that I no longer have anything to fear.[2] For those of us in Christ Jesus, *we* no longer have anything to fear.

We no longer fear death because, to be absent from the body, is to be *home* with Jesus Christ.[3] As the Apostle Paul said, "to live is Christ and to die is gain."[4] In life, we live for Christ by honoring Him in all we do. In death, leaving our earthly bodies, we gain the full and uninterrupted presence of Jesus Christ.[5] While on earth, we temporarily lose connection with our loved ones who have gone to be with the Lord. Yet in death, we gain by uniting with them once again. In life and death, in Christ Jesus, *we win.*

Our New Bodies

Dorothy is no longer in Kansas, and we are clearly no longer in the Garden of Eden. Since the fall of humankind, we live in a world that has fallen under the curse of sin and death. This world is no longer God's perfectly created Garden of Eden where the vegetation is perfect and lush; but rather, this earth is prone to decay, thorns, and thistles.[6] Health issues occur in this fallen world. Cancer. Lung disease. Heart disease. Even cleft lip and palate.

While learning about life after death, I found hope even in the midst of our fallen world where health issues occur. I can live well in my current body because I know that a body with a cleft lip and palate is not the end of the story. Although we may grow weary in our present bodies, for those in Christ Jesus, when we die and leave this earthly body, we will be given a new and eternal body made for us by God himself.[7]

The new and glorious body I will receive after death on Earth fills my heart with anticipation. Just in my early thirties, I can already feel the effects of the aging process. As a child, I never stretched before an athletic contest. Now, I have to stretch multiple times before going for a leisurely run. It doesn't take long for our earthly bodies to reveal that they aren't going to last forever. Although I can still physically do most of what I did as a youth (I'm just extremely sore the next couple of days), it was an elderly man who opened my eyes to the desire to put on our new bodies.

Matching stride for stride as we walked down the hallway towards the same destination, this man smirked and said, "Wanna race? I bet I can beat you!" After a quick laugh, he soberly shared that he whole-heartedly desired to run again. He desired to run as fast as he did in his youth but stated, "My mind says I can, but my body tells me, 'No you can't.'"

His mind still wanted to run. He remembered the feeling of pushing himself past physical exhaustion in his youth, but here in his early 80s, he felt the same desire to run—only his physical body would no longer allow him to. As a former athlete, this man wanted to move in a way that he could before, without pain or the fear of breaking a bone.

Paul well understood this man's dilemma. He was tired of the physical limitations of his aging body. It was not that he did not want a body. Rather, he wanted his perishable body to be swallowed up by life![8] How exciting for the believer in Christ, knowing that one day in our new and glorious body, we will be able to run again for all of eternity without any limitations. Our new eternal bodies will be indestructible[9] and will never grow weak, wear out, or experience pain. Even in the prime of life, when our bodies are strong, fast and pain free, our earthly bodies will in no way compare to what is yet to come. For all of eternity, we will be in bodies that will allow us to do more than what our minds here on earth could ever imagine. For all of eternity, our minds will tell us we can run, and our bodies will be in full agreement.

The Question

Learning about the new and glorious eternal body I will one day receive excited me. It really did. It filled me with hope. But like most things, I didn't fully comprehend it all at once. I still had more to learn. I remember the day like yesterday, sitting in my friend's living room, excited to share my "new revelation." Although it was blistery cold outside, I was warm with a blanket on my lap, sipping hot chocolate in hand, and a fire of excitement within me.

"Okay; guess what I figured out?!" I exclaimed.

A little suspicious of my excitement and unwilling to blindly drink the Kool-Aid, she cautiously asked, "What have you 'figured out'?"

Feeling overly confident, I naively jumped in the deep water with both feet.

"So, you know how God has created us in our mother's womb and He doesn't make mistakes?"

"Yeah," She responded.

"And you know how when Christ returns, we're going to get new and glorious eternal bodies?!"

Still not matching my excitement and growing more suspicious, she gave a simple *yep* head nod.

Reaching the peak of my excitement, I exclaimed, "Well, that's all true; but since I have a cleft lip and palate that resulted from environmental or genetic issues from living in this fallen world, I don't think God cares about my body at all. This body is pretty much *junk*. I mean, when I die, I will get a brand-new body anyway. God cares about my heart, but He certainly doesn't care about this body."

Looking back toward my friend, I expected to find her in awe of my new revelation. Although her mouth was hanging wide open, it was not a "Wow, your 'revelation' blew my mind" kind of jaw-dropping experience. With a dumbfounded, *Are you serious?* questioning look, silence weighed heavy upon the room as she gathered her thoughts.

Shaking her head, she finally muttered, "No. Sorry; but you're wrong. God cares about your body. It's not a mistake. It's certainly not *junk*. He cares about all of our bodies. He created all of us for a purpose. You need to see what God's Word says about your body."

I thought that because I was born with a cleft lip and palate, God no longer cared about my physical body and was just going to replace it with a new one. It was a good attempt at trying to make God more like me. I didn't like my body, so I didn't think He should either. I incorrectly believed environmental or genetic factors "ruined" my body, and therefore, God didn't care about it anymore. Thankfully, my friend pointed out my faulty and unbiblical thinking. Although I passionately believed what I was saying at the time, my friend was wise in many ways. I had no choice but to stop and seriously consider her response. Was I incorrect to think that my body was ruined? Was she correct that my body was *not* junk?

Soon after, God began to reveal and unravel the lies. He taught me that although the fall of humankind does affect our physical bodies, sin didn't derail God's plan to renew our physical bodies to make them whole and complete. And God continues to carry out His plan of redemption, never allowing this fallen world to disqualify His love, tenderness, and involvement in every detail of creation—including my earthly body.

Transformed Bodies

Transformed. The word was a game-changer for me. Listening to his sermon, "The Ultimate 'Extreme Makeover,'" Dr. David Jeremiah explained our new bodies in a way I had never understood.[10] Shortly after my conversation with my friend, I learned that God would not be abandoning my earthly body in the grave and starting over with a brand new one. Rather He would *transform* my current body into my new and glorious eternal body.

Transform.

A caterpillar transforms into a butterfly.

Our earthly bodies transform into new and glorious ones.

Our new and glorious bodies are not separate from our current bodies.

Rather, they are a *continuum* of our current body.

To understand the continuum of our earthly bodies into our new and glorious bodies, let's consider the Apostle Paul's analogy of our earthly body being like a seed. In First Corinthians, Paul teaches us that our earthly bodies are like "seeds," which are buried or "planted" in the ground when we pass from this life to our eternal one. With our earthly bodies buried in the cemetery upon our death, they become like seeds in the ground, ready to spring forth-new life upon Christ's return.[11]

Although the seed determines the kind of plant that grows, the plant appears much different from the seed. A rose seed, for example, will look much different from the rose it grows into; yet the seed is such an essential step to create the beautiful flower. The seed is as much a part of the rose as the delicate petals and wonderful smell. Without it, a radiant rose would not bloom.

In the same way, our earthly bodies are as much a part of God's plan of redemption. In death, our earthly bodies will be planted into the ground. In resurrection, our glorious bodies will spring forth. These bodies will be different and better than our current bodies but will still be "identifiable as belonging to the same person."[12]

We can learn so much about our own bodily resurrection from Christ's resurrection. Just as Jesus' body was raised from the dead, so will every believer in Christ be raised.[13] After returning from the dead, Jesus said to His disciples, "Look at my hands. Look at my feet. You can see that it's really me."[14] Just as Jesus was still Jesus after the resurrection, you will *forever* be you. Just as the disciples recognized Jesus in His new and resurrected body, we too will recognize others, and they will recognize us.[15]

Consider with me for a second.

Our bodies will be raised in glorious form; but we will still be ourselves. Not only is there only one of you on planet Earth at this very moment, but there has never been another like you nor will there ever be. God loves you so much that He created you so intentionally; there will only ever be one of *you* in all of eternity.

God did not handcraft us in our mother's womb just to forget about our bodies when we die. No. He has a plan. He will redeem each of our bodies. How exciting! Even as humans, we share in His joy of restoration. We take joy in using our hands to restore old things. Our hearts rejoice when we see the old home remodeled into the dream home. We enjoy seeing that old Mustang restored to its former glory, cruising the country roads on a Sunday afternoon. Yet our bodies are not left to earthly makeup artists; they're left to the *Creator* of the makeup artists—the Creator of every living being, canyon, and cloud—every intricate masterpiece.

God is the original restorer.

Restoration and *renewal* are His very nature.

He restores broken hearts and brings us fresh hope once again.

He renews our hearts and minds to think and see things as He does.

Thinking back to the conversation with my friend, I humbly stand corrected. While our earthly bodies are not yet in perfect form, they are not junk. Think about it, what do you do with garbage? What do you do with the old television or computer? When something is no longer of use, many of us throw it in the landfill. We bury it deep and never think about it again. After all, it has become junk to us—meaningless and replaceable with no additional purpose.

In His amazing plan of redemption, God does not disregard our earthly bodies in the grave as if they do not matter or have no value. God refuses to destroy our bodies because He *uniquely* formed us. He created us to be irreplaceable. One of a kind. He doesn't forget about our bodies because when He called His creation *very good*, He actually meant it.

I no longer fear death because I have learned that death is not the end.

I recall visiting my grandfather's grave and seeing the flowers and flags adorn the tombstones, making what could have been a rather depressing sight beautiful. It was in that moment that I understood the importance of valuing and respecting an individual's physical body in death. Why should we respect the physical remains of someone after they pass away? Because God purposefully created everything about that person, even their physical body. Our bodies matter to God, and they should matter to us. In my mind, a graveyard was once a depressive picture of people who once walked the earth; and now I view it as a beautiful image of the resting place for those who will always be and will once again be raised in the fullness of life.

Oh. What hope we have in Jesus!

Living with the End in Mind

Although I laugh at my crazy fears now, the childhood fear of death actually taught me to live this life well with the end in mind. Living with the end in mind reminds me that the current death rate is 100%. We will *all* die and face eternity.

Living with the end in mind is like an Olympic runner who disciplines herself physically and mentally in preparation for a race of a lifetime. She trains in hopes that she will reach the finish line and behold the prize. However, all the conditioning, healthy eating, and mental preparation is all for nothing if the runner fails to set her eyes upon the finish line. If the runner doesn't know where she is headed, how can she reach her ultimate destination? A runner who competes doesn't stare at the ground in front of her but rather *lifts her eyes* and sets them straight toward her goal. With her head up, she runs the race with every ounce of energy left within her.

Simply, she runs the race to *win*.

I want to run the race of life in this earthly body just like that—with my eyes up, looking ahead to the finish line, emptying out all that is within me. My goal: to win the prize that does not perish but rather a prize that will last forever.[16] Even as I write these words, conviction reminds me that too often, instead of having my eyes up and gathered in running position, I find myself sitting at the starting line, sulking in my insecurities of being born with a cleft lip and palate. When I find myself sulking, I simply need to *lift my eyes* and start running again. I desperately want to run the race of life towards my eternal home with Christ Jesus.

Rather than being hyper focused on asking God *why* I was born with a cleft lip and palate, I'm learning to simply run the race of life towards Him, regardless of how I was knitted together in my mother's womb. Lifting my eyes up, I see that this body in which I currently live, this body I can touch and feel, is not the end of the story.

While our Christian walk isn't easy, it's always characterized by *hope*. In hope, I can look past the here and now and consider that this life is not the only one I will live.

The best is yet to come.

Never again will we face the challenging situations that we face while living on this earth. We won't have any issues with our eternal bodies. That is a money-back guarantee. With that in mind, right now, as long as we have breath in our lungs, we have a chance to honor God on this side of heaven, using our current bodies. While we're alive, we have the opportunity to learn to embrace our bodies, talents, and unique qualities, choosing to not pick apart our appearances or abilities, but rather trust in God's good plan for the *creation and redemption* of our earthly bodies. With the hope of eternity in front of me, I want to honor God in all things, including my cleft lip and palate.

With my eyes up, I keep my current body and cleft in the proper perspective. Rather than become consumed by my physical appearance, I'm learning to take a step back and look through the wide-angled lens and see my earthly body in a whole new way. So what is the role of our earthly bodies? How should we see and treat our earthly body?

A Temporary Residence

Since we have been saved, we're to wait with eager hope, great confidence, and patience for our new bodies.[17] God's Word does not tell us to wait for our transformed bodies begrudgingly, irritably, and self-conscious of our every flaw. However, I have to admit—even now, at times, I still struggle to like my earthly body as much as God does. When I struggle to like my body, I recall the Apostle Paul's comparison of our earthly bodies to "tents."[18] A tent signifies a *temporary* residence. The focus of a tent isn't its outward appearance but rather the purpose and function.

Arriving in sunny Moab, Utah, my friend Aubrie and I quickly set up our campsite and ventured out for a short hike before sundown. With the beaming sun out and no rain in sight, we decided to leave the cover off of the tent so it could air out while we were away. Midway into our hike, the sun suddenly fell behind the clouds. Large droplets of rain slowly began to fall.

Unaware of the drastic weather changes that can occur at higher altitudes, we ventured on without a care in the world. Quickly, the sprinkle became a downpour. We were soaking wet. Soon, small streams of water rolled over the rock formations in the distance. With the rocks becoming slippery, a more experienced group of hikers assisted us to higher ground as we found shelter under the ledge of a huge rock. We quickly made friends as we packed ourselves in the only small dry area that remained.

As we sat and waited out the downpour, our new friends shared stories of their previous hiking experiences. While listening to their stories, my adrenaline was finally calming, and I breathed a deep crisis-avoided sigh of relief. Although we didn't know when the rain would stop, we were now in a dry and safe place. One person was even starting to pass around some food and drinks! I knew we were in good hands! Although not an ideal situation, I relaxed, knowing that the rain would eventually pass, and we would make it back to our campsite.

Wait!

Our campsite!

We had left the tent uncovered, and it was pouring down rain! Nudging my friend who was talking with the other hikers, I exclaimed, "We left the tent open! Our sleeping bags and pillows *have* to be soaked!" Exhausted from a long day of travel, the last thing I wanted to do was dry our sleeping gear. At this point, I just wanted to get myself dry, warm, and go to bed!

Within a half hour, the rain had stopped. As we returned to the campsite, we enthusiastically found that although our campsite was less than 1 mile away from where we hiked, it never rained near our tent. Although we were cold and soaking wet, our tent was dry!

I now understand Paul's comparison to our earthly bodies as tents. When we returned to our tent that evening, we wanted to know one thing: Would our tent serve its purpose of sheltering us and allow us to get a good night's rest? We were not concerned about having the most beautiful and magnificent tent. When we returned, we weren't comparing our tent to our neighbor's tent. We simply wanted our temporary dwelling to serve its purpose by giving us a dry place to sleep at night.

I know I'm not the only one who cares more about the function of a tent than the appearance. Often times, after a rainy or windy night, the topic of discussion with other campers is, "Did you stay dry last night?" and, "Did your tent withstand the strong winds?" These concerns are unrelated to appearance and prestige; but rather, the focus is on *purpose* and *function*.

When we understand our earthly bodies as tents, our temporary residences rather than our forever homes, we keep a proper perspective. Understanding that our earthly bodies are temporary doesn't mean we don't maintain our appearance and steward our bodies. Healthy eating, exercise, and adequate rest become important to us, as we want to steward this gift that God has given us while on this earth. Just as we would tend to our tents with patches when worn, we want our earthly bodies to be as strong as possible to weather the storms and function to the best of their abilities.

Understanding our earthly bodies as temporary dwellings simply reminds us of our bigger purpose. We are reminded to not allow ourselves to be consumed with our physical appearances. Knowing that God loves our bodies and will one day restore them with no sign of the aging process,[19] we don't need to become frantic about every wrinkle and ounce of weight gain. With the proper perspective, we no longer make our bodies the source of our value and worth. Seeing our earthly bodies as temporary, we no longer make our physical make-up the focus of our earthly existence.

Realizing our bodies are like tents does not mean we deny that *we are beautiful.* We don't have to respond with "What?!? This ole thang?" each time someone compliments us on our physical appearance. Clearly, we're beautiful, as God designed us with His own hands. Of that, we can be sure. Knowing our bodies are not junk and without value, we can live well. We use our whole body to do what is right for the glory of God, not allowing any part of our body to become an instrument of evil.[20]

Our Bodies Are Instruments to Glorify God

In the times when we don't like our bodies, it helps to remember that they're not our own. They're not ours to dislike. Our bodies have been bought with a price and were given to us so that we may honor God.[21] Our lives have been claimed for the glory of Christ, and everything we do should honor and glorify God.[22] We were created by God and for Him.[23] As believers in Christ, we are to give our bodies to God in worship as a living and holy sacrifice.[24]

Rather than focus on the things we like or dislike about ourselves, we lay our bodies at the feet of Jesus, giving our *entire* being to God. We give Him our heart. Our mind. Our will. Our emotions. We present to Him our physical bodies and ask Him to use our bodies as an instrument for good.

I used to tell God that I didn't like how big my hands and feet were; but now I'm learning to simply ask Him to use my hands and feet to honor and glorify Him. I have been gifted hands, not to pick apart and loath the size of them, but to be the hands of Jesus to those around me. I have been gifted feet, not to complain about how I wish they would fit into prettier shoes but to be the feet of Jesus, bringing the Good News of Jesus Christ to those around me. When I struggle with the shape of my nose, I remember I have been gifted a nose that allows me to smell the roses and appreciate the beauty that God has bestowed to us and praise Him for His wonderful works. Whatever God has given me; I want to use it for His glory.

Some are born with birth defects. Yet some suffer physical hardships in the form of childhood accidents. I have the blessing of personally knowing two individuals who suffered physical loss in this world, yet they choose to honor God and glorify His name in the midst. One young man, who had his foot amputated at the age of three due to a lawn mower accident, is now in graduate school studying to be a prosthetist so that he may make prosthetic limbs for those who have suffered similar losses. A young woman, who became a quadriplegic in a car accident at the age of five, now serves as a social worker at a local hospital. Her desire is to help others. She gives everything she has, even employing an assistant to help carry out the daily requirements of the job, so she can help others in their time of need.

From the outside looking in, I see much good in their lives. Both of them could have chosen anger, bitterness, and resentment for the situations that they were dealt. They could have turned inward and wallowed in self-pity and feelings of despair. Instead, they have allowed God to produce good fruit through their lives. Because of their daily choices to make the most of their physical abilities, they have done much good in others' lives.

The young woman cannot walk; but she is using her body to glorify God by using the brain He has blessed her with to help coordinate care for others. The young man doesn't have his foot; but he is using the hands God has gifted him to create prosthetic limbs for others so they, too, can overcome their physical limitations.

These two serve as a personal encouragement to me. They remind me that, although we live in a fallen world where birth defects and injury are possible, if we allow God, He will work all situations for our good and His glory. Like them, we can choose to look past our physical limitations, instead focusing on our physical *abilities* and utilizing them for the welfare of those around us.

When I think about my cleft lip and palate in light of eternity with Christ, it seems so minor. Thinking about the transformation of this earthly body into a glorious new eternal body, I cannot help but look at the shape of my nose and the surgeries it required and feel it's so trivial in the scope of eternity where every wrong will be made right. When I consider every old thing in this fleeting world made new for all of eternity, my cleft lip and palate seems insignificant. Understanding that the best is yet to come helps me live well in my current body.

CHAPTER 9

Living as an Anomaly

"The fact that I am a woman does not make me a different kind of Christian, but the fact that I am a Christian does make me a different kind of woman."

- Elisabeth Elliot

Even in my early years, I was cognizant that I appeared different from others. As early as five years of age, I began to overhear a few curious kids ask their mothers, "What happened to that little girl's nose?" I recall one instance while shopping with my mom. Sensing the stares of another child who was located within a few feet of me, I promptly hid to get out of view. Within a few moments, my mom found me and ushered me out from behind the clothes rack. Although I no longer hide from strangers in stores, there have been plenty of instances when my cleft lip and palate has made me feel *different from others.*

After one surgery during my freshman year of high school, the doctor expressed concern that I risked an opponent hitting me in the face with an elbow while playing basketball. He feared someone might break my nose, which he had just repaired. The recovery process interrupted my normal routine, as it sidelined me from playing the sport I loved. After adequate time to heal, the doctor cleared me to play again, but with one condition: unlike my teammates, he wanted me to wear a protective facemask.

When my mom showed me a picture of the facemask in a shopping catalog, with one look, I immediately knew I was *not* wearing that.

Oh this mask.

Let me just say they call it a *facemask* for a reason.

This mask was clear in color, covered the majority of the face, and had two huge black Velcro straps that secured it around the head. Honestly, I never even considered trying to play basketball in that big bulky thing. If the doctor asked me to wear it for a week, I may have done it. However, to be the only one wearing a huge mask each time I played basketball would be a constant reminder that I was *different*.

There were other situations that made me feel different from others as well. During Christmas break of my senior year of college, the doctor took a bone graft from my hip and placed it in the front of my mouth so dental implants could be anchored. While doing this procedure, he also completed a scar revision of my lip, which required many stitches. Being self-conscious and not wanting stares and questions from strangers, I confined myself to my house.

Normally an active person, I disliked being inside for too long and became incredibly stir crazy. Although I didn't want to be seen by the general public, I needed human interaction and felt most comfortable with my family. Not having left the house for a few days, and during Christmas season nonetheless, I was more excited than ever to go to our extended-family Christmas party. I eagerly anticipated *this specific* Christmas party, as I could taste the freedom of leaving the house and was excited to gain a little bit of normalcy once again.

During my college years, my siblings and I played table games and socialized with our same-aged cousins. This Christmas was no different. While enjoying good conversation, my brother made a funny remark, and immediately, the whole group began laughing. It was not the cordial, "Wow, that isn't really funny but I better laugh anyway" kind of laughter. This was the "I'm gonna choke on my water or spit it out" uncontrolled, deep belly laughter.

In a spontaneous response to his hilarious comment, my lips quickly retracted in the form of a smile and laughter came forth out of my mouth. I immediately felt the stretching of my upper lip where the stitches held the skin secure. It *hurt*! I quickly grabbed the sides of my upper lip and held them tight while the pain settled my laughter. Irritated at the pain and my inability to laugh freely, I couldn't help but become frustrated.

I thought, "I just want to be *normal*." You know, doing the *normal* things like sharing a laugh with friends. Doing *normal* things like freely leaving the house instead of being cooped up all week. *Normal* things—like eating delicious Christmas cookies instead of drinking endless chocolate Boost, as I still couldn't eat solid foods while my incisions healed. In many ways, my cleft lip and palate seemed to disrupt the normal flow of my life.

What is Normal?

Growing up, whenever I commented about my nose looking "flat" or "different," my dad would tell me that my nose looked just like his. He would say, "Your nose looks like just the rest of the Verhoff pugged noses. I have one too." Shaking my head in disbelief, I quickly dismissed his words. I responded, "Um…no dad. No."

Looking back on this vulnerable season in my life, I wish I wouldn't have feared or avoided being different. I now appreciate the perspective that he offered. I have to admit, I have seen a great variety of shapes of noses and have yet to figure out which shape is "normal." Looking back, that was my dad's point. Across all nationalities and ethnicities that God created, there have been a vast array of noses—all unique. How could we call one shape or size *normal*?

As I have matured, I have come to understand that these differences are what make us beautiful, as God handcrafted each of us as one-of-a-kind. Honestly, I think that is why God made us all so different and unique—so we can learn to appreciate the beauty in our uniqueness rather than waste our energy trying to be just like everyone else. God created us all so different that there is no such thing as "normal." Being normal is not a concern of God and, therefore, should not be a concern of mine.

Being a follower of Christ isn't just for Americans. Christianity is a religion that started in the Middle East with the Israelites and has spread throughout the nations as God's message of salvation is for *all people*. Jesus Christ did not shed His blood for people who look, act, and speak like me. Jesus' shed blood has ransomed people from every tribe, language, and nation.[1] For eternity, heaven will be comprised of people from all different nationalities, races, and ethnicities. Here on earth today and for all of eternity, God has made His people different.

Different skin colors.

Different body types.

Different facial features.

Different eye color.

Different hair color and styles.

Even different shapes of noses.

All of these individuals make up the diversity of God's people.

All these individuals will make up the diversity of heaven.

For all of eternity, we may look different, but we will all be there for the *same* reason, to place our attention and affection on the King of kings and Lord of lords. Our physical differences are not to be the center of attention; Jesus is. Rather than focus on how we're different, we can look at everyone we meet and recognize that, though they might be physically or mentally different from us, God loves us all the same.[2] Knowing He loves us the same, we can look at others and recognize that they are God's prized possessions, created for a purpose and deeply loved by Him. There is nothing wrong with those born lacking physical or mental perfection; and if we fail to see the beauty in them, the wrong is simply in our view.

A Beauty That Never Fades

God surely finds our physical differences beautiful. While God has created each person unique with physical beauty, He finds a greater beauty within us that never ages, never fades, and is renewed day by day.[3] This true beauty is the inner transformation of our hearts and minds as we become more like Him.

Our measure of life isn't in the vibrancy of our skin, our toned athletic muscles, or physical endurance of our youth. Our measure of life is how we allow our inward person in Christ to grow and transform. In the midst of our aging physical bodies, in Christ our spirit thrives more and more. When our earthly bodies deteriorate with age, we're simply reminded to fix our eyes on those things that will last forever.[4]

Our beauty should not come from outward adornment but rather come from within—the unfading beauty of a gentle and quiet spirit, which is so precious to God.[5] Rather than scratching and clawing to achieve every standard of earthly beauty, I rest in knowing that, while man looks at the outer appearance, God looks at the heart.[6] True beauty is a heart that bows to the name of Jesus and is demonstrated through a genuine love and concern for others.

While God has created beautiful physical bodies as well, our primary focus becomes our inward beauty, our spiritual renewal in Christ. I am learning to see differently. When I see others, and myself, I want to see the inward person before I see the external appearance. I want to focus most on the condition of my heart and my obedience to God's Word.

Being "normal" is no longer my aim in this life. No longer am

I concerned that the shape of my nose is different from others; my focus is being the kind of different God has called me to be. I'm not talking about dyeing my hair purple with pink polka dots just for the sake of being "different." I'm talking about the life-changing difference of being a follower of Christ. I'm talking about an inner transformation that resembles the heart of Christ.[7]

Becoming Like Him

Doctor appointments and surgeries can provoke great fear in children. My brother and I were cautious when visiting the doctor. My brother was especially anxious when nurses and doctors were in his presence. While in the post-op room following a surgery, his heart rate monitor began beeping. Growing concerned, the medical team tried to calm him.

Although it was not yet time for my parents to come back and see him, being unsuccessful in their attempts, they called my parents from the waiting room to see if they could settle him. With the medical staff out of the room, shortly his heart rate lowered and the heart monitor stopped beeping. After a few minutes, a nurse walked back in the room and the monitor went off again. For a young boy, her mere presence was enough to create an anxious heart!

To help decrease anxiety before doctor appointments, my mom explained to us what the nice man in the suit and tie was going to do. I soon learned that each time I visited Dr. Robinson, he was working to repair my nose and lip. With each visit, he completed a different step of the process. One visit he straightened the lip and cleaned up scar tissue. The next visit, he added a bone graft to add height and dimension to my nose. Throughout the years, through a gradual process of change, Dr. Robinson built my nose and restored my lip—and our fear of doctors slowly decreased.

As I flip through my school pictures, with each passing year, I see a transformation. There was the typical development that everyone experiences: the awkward body changes of junior high. You know, the reason we hide the yearbook and pray none of our classmates have pictures *or* memories of us.

In addition, my pictures reveal physical changes with each surgery. In early pictures, I had many missing teeth. In more recent, I had fake teeth that filled the gaps. Many years of wearing braces aligned my natural teeth before permanent teeth were implanted. In early pictures, my nose looks flatter. In later photos, many do not even recognize I was born with a cleft lip and palate. Regardless of what others see in my pictures today, I remember it as a continuum—a process that did not occur over night. One-step. Then another. Little by little, my physical transformation took place.

Just as the physical repairing of a bilateral cleft lip and palate is a process of change that doesn't happen overnight, so is our transformation of becoming like Christ. As a surgeon takes the nose with a flattened appearance and uses bone grafts to build the nose up, he must always remember that he's building a nose. As believers in Christ, we, too, must remember what we're building and reshaping ourselves into—and we must allow the best doctor of all to help transform us: Jesus.

Instead of merely fixing up our exterior, we should honestly evaluate the condition of our heart and determine who we are *really* becoming. Are we building a self-centered existence or are we learning to be concerned about the welfare of others? Are our own desires and dreams our top priority or have we willingly laid our dreams and desires into His hands? Are we building a life focused on the fleeting things of this world, or are we building our lives on the Rock of Jesus Christ?

In Christ, I'm becoming different.

In a way only He can, Christ transforms our dead hearts and brings them to life. As Ezekiel saw the valley of dry bones and raised them to life, so does the Lord place His life-giving Spirit within us so that we may truly live.[8] He removes our stony and stubborn hearts and gives us hearts that are tender and responsive to Him.[9] No longer giving our sinful fleshly desires reign over our lives, we allow His indwelling nature within us to be outwardly expressed in our lives.[10]

Bearing Fruit

I love peaches. One early September evening, my friend Aubrie and I stopped at an orchard to pick some fresh peaches. This was a little different from the orchards we were used to seeing in Ohio. This day, we were visiting Capitol Reef National Park in Utah. Cooled by the late summer breeze, a sense of peace and contentment swept over me as I admired the rock formations in the near distance.

The scenery felt like we were transported back in time to the late 1800s. The orchard was located near a weathered barn with old worn, wooden fencing outlining the pasture that once contained the livestock of the early settlers. The orchard, which was a source of sustenance and profit for those who planted, quickly became a highlight of our trip as I literally enjoyed the fruits of their labor.

This orchard was an open orchard, meaning that we were allowed to roam inside and sample the fruit. With my love for peaches, merely sampling the fruit was not an option. I already knew I was going to devour more than my share, so I had better pay in advance. After paying for the peaches, we walked around the orchard, finding the best peaches and ate until our hearts' content. Even as I retell the experience, my mouth waters. I can almost taste them. Did I mention I love peaches? Honestly, I ate far too many. They were *so* good.

More than I want to enjoy the pleasurable experience of eating fresh fruit, I want the Lord to be pleased with the fruit of my abiding with Him. Just as the peach trees were full of delicious fruit, our lives should be full of the good fruit of being in relationship with Him. We abide. We remain in a permanent relationship with Him. In doing so, we grow. We change. We bear much fruit.[11]

We cannot live righteously by our own good works. We don't transform to be like Christ by our own attempts to be moral. In fact, our efforts to obtain righteousness are like filthy rags.[12] Becoming like Him is not like a New Year's Resolution or the turning over of a new leaf in which we *strive* on our own effort to make ourselves better. No. We can't do it on our own.

Becoming like Christ is an inside-out transformation that only the power of the Holy Spirit within us can accomplish. Our position is not one of working to try to clean up our exterior, but it's one of continual abiding in the presence of God, asking the Holy Spirit to do His work within our hearts.

After spending time in the Word, prayer, and fellowship with God's people, we look back and realize that we're far more patient than when we were first planted in our relationship with Christ. Although we're far from perfect, little by little, we worry less and trust Him more. He prunes away fits of anger, jealousy, and envy, as those are not characteristics of the Vine and therefore should not be within the branch.

It's not by our own power and will but the work of the Holy Spirit that regenerates our hearts and transforms our nature to be like Him. With the Master Gardener tending to me, He prunes the fruit bearing branches so that they produce even more.[13] When we remain in this life-giving connection to the Vine, good fruit is the product. Being *different* is the ultimate result.

The Kind of Different I Want to Be

As I scroll through an old Speech-Language Pathology textbook, I'm reminded that a cleft lip and palate is also known as a type of *craniofacial anomaly.* "Craniofacial anomalies are a diverse group of deformities in the growth of the head and facial bones. *Anomaly* is a medical term meaning 'irregularity' or 'different from normal.'"[14]

In a world of political correctness and amidst attempts to avoid any possible offensive language, the word *anomaly* could be a word that some find offensive. After all, who wants to be...different?

The answer to that question is simple: As believers in Christ, it should be the utmost desire of our hearts. I actually appreciate this terminology, as it helped me receive the medical treatment that I needed. Furthermore, it reminds me that as a Christian, I should be radically different from the norm.

"Different from normal."

I like that.

While reading the Book of Ruth, God impressed upon my heart two characteristics of Ruth that I should desire to make the hallmark of my life. Although I'm a work in progress, my prayer is that God would change me to walk in *everyday faithfulness* and develop a *virtuous character* as Ruth displayed.

Ruth and Orpah were the daughters-in-law of Naomi. Naomi's husband and two sons died, leaving all three woman widowed. The women were living in Moab. During this time, Naomi heard the Lord blessed the people in Judah by giving them good crops again. Returning to Naomi's homeland, Naomi, Ruth, and Orpah set off for Bethlehem. Soon after they departed, Naomi told her daughters-in-law to remain in Moab so the Lord could provide them with the security of another marriage. Despite her mother-in-law's request for her to go back to her homeland, Ruth "clung tightly to Naomi."[15]

The Hebrew verb for "clung tightly" emphasizes Ruth's love for Naomi. This word is used to describe a man being *joined to* his wife and a person *staying faithful to the Lord*.[16] Certain that she would go with her mother-in-law, Ruth boldly replied, "Don't ask me to leave you and turn back. Wherever you go, I will go; wherever you live, I will live. Your people will be my people and your God will be my God. Wherever you die, I will die and there I will be buried."[17]

With commitment equivalent to marriage, she said, *till death do us part*. Ruth was committed to stand with Naomi and turn from the pagan gods of Moab to serve the One True God. Ruth verbalized a constant and abiding allegiance to her mother-in-law and God. This is faithfulness.

After arriving in Bethlehem, Ruth continued to demonstrate

everyday faithfulness. She took the initiative to go out and harvest stalks of grain left behind by the harvesters to provide Naomi with food. It was this everyday faithfulness that grabbed the attention of Boaz as he heard about everything Ruth had done for her mother-in-law.[18] When Ruth asked Boaz to be her family redeemer, Boaz responded by affirming Ruth's loyalty to her family and told her to not worry about a thing, as he would do whatever was necessary. After all, everyone in town knew Ruth was a virtuous woman.[19]

Ruth was not marked by her marital status, her career choice, or her physical appearance; rather, she was marked by being a virtuous woman. In our culture, it's easy for us to seek the blessing and prosperity of God more than we seek obtaining the character of God.

Ruth's love was sacrificial, as she demonstrated faithfulness to Naomi, regardless of what she could get in return. Ruth was not promised that staying with her mother-in-law and following God would result in a family redeemer. She did not ask, "What is in this for me?" when she made the decision to be faithful to her mother-in-law and care for her with generosity. Ruth was faithful to her mother-in-law and left the results of her faithfulness up to God.

Ruth was a world-changer and didn't even know it. Ruth's decision of everyday faithfulness changed the world forever, as her faithful actions caught the attention of Boaz and Jesus Christ was ultimately born through her linage.

When we live out everyday faithfulness, we go against the status quo and popular opinion and follow God and His Word at all costs. In our everyday faithfulness, we do not have to wait for the "big events" of our lives in order to make a difference. We don't have to lead droves of people to Christ in a remote village, stand in front of a large crowd spreading the Gospel, or be a worship leader in a world-renowned praise-and-worship band in order to change the world. While these are larger-known evangelical (and powerful) ways to serve the masses, they're not a requirement to be a world changer. As Ruth demonstrated, the world is not always changed through grandiose and entertaining Christian events; but rather, the world is changed when God's people commit to an everyday faithfulness to the God they claim to serve.

Do you want to make a difference in this world?

Be faithful.

Be a faithful friend.

A faithful parent.

A faithful spouse.

A faithful son or daughter.

Above all, be faithful to God.

As we wake up each morning and humble ourselves before God, we ask that He walk with us and guide our hearts, minds, and actions. It's when we choose *each day* to surrender ourselves before the Lord that our *entire* life will be His. When we exhibit faithfulness each day, we build faithful lives.

In a world full of self-centeredness, the Christian walk truly is an anomaly. Living in everyday faithfulness to God and those around us is contrary to the majority. In a world where we're quick to shut out others if they even slightly offend us, everyday faithfulness is a true commodity.

In everyday faithfulness, our actions speak louder than our words; and others see that our entire lives, even the most mundane jobs, have been transformed by the saving grace of Jesus Christ. In everyday faithfulness, others will see that our faith is genuine and they may actually be *compelled* to listen to us when we speak of Jesus Christ.

I now see the beauty of different.

I don't want to stay the same.

I want God to transform my heart and continue to make me more and more like Him.

I want to be different.

Less of me. Far more of Him.

Thank God, for the *difference* that only Jesus Christ can make in our lives.

CHAPTER 10

Working All Things for Good

"Look for yourself and you will find loneliness and despair. But look for Christ and you will find Him and everything else."

- C.S. Lewis

The perspective in which we choose to view life situations is a huge part of our success in overcoming personal challenges. At the end of my senior year of college, I was scheduled to have a scar revision to soften its appearance. During the months leading up, I found myself focusing more and more on my scars, wondering what the revision would look like.

One evening after practice, I showered in the locker room before heading home. As I passed the bathroom mirror, I looked over my left shoulder and caught a glimpse of my reflection. With concerns for the upcoming surgery weighing on me, I stared at myself and began to think about the changes that would appear after the surgery. After standing there for a few moments, I was quickly brought back to reality when I heard my teammates snickering, asking if everything was all right.

Even after the surgery, I spent a lot of time looking at the scars in the mirror. When I looked at my reflection, I found my eyes gazing directly to the scars on my lip. Soon it became a habit. They became the first thing I saw when looking in the mirror to get ready in the morning; and they were the last thing I looked at when getting ready for bed.

Do you know what happens when you look for your scars each time you look in the mirror?

You find them.

You see, when we're hyper-focused on what we believe to be our flaws, we will find them each time we look. In a selfie generation, focusing on every suspected flaw and placing a filter on what we do not like is more prevalent than ever. By taking our focus off what we believe to be our physical flaws, we can step back and see the bigger picture.

Approximately four years ago while hiking, God taught me that I needed to see the bigger picture of His creation, rather than focus on what I believe to be flawed. Ascending the winding trail, I kept my eyes on the ground in front of me, ensuring I wouldn't trip over the large tree roots and rocks that were scattered on top of the dirt. I focused my eyes on the path because my legs were getting tired, and there wasn't much scenery to enjoy anyway. I knew we were nearing the highest point, but all I could see around me were the overgrown brush and trees that lined both sides of the trail. It felt like we had been walking in unending woods for hours, yet I knew we had to be getting closer to the top.

As I neared the peak of the trail, I turned to the right and suddenly found myself standing near the edge of the cliff. I had made it to the top and felt the sun on my face for the first time since I started the hike. Although the hours of hiking left me questioning why this hike was so popular, now overlooking the meadow below, I understood. It was the most breathtaking scenic view I have ever witnessed. The trees were a lush green, the sky was blue, and the sun was radiantly shining deep in the valley. The scenery looked picture perfect. Flawless. I could have stared at it forever.

I took many pictures that day. After returning home from vacation and looking through my pictures, I noticed something I hadn't noticed while overlooking the meadow. In the midst of this incredible scenery, there dwelled one dead tree in the midst of the countless beautiful thriving ones. What was once a memory of such a beautiful landscape now lost its beauty, as all I could focus on was this *one* lifeless tree, even though so much vibrant life and beauty surrounded it. I couldn't look past the *one thing* that I didn't find beautiful.

That dead tree.

I could not take my eyes off of it.

Struggling to see the life that surrounded the withered tree, I realized that I was pitifully good at picking things apart and focusing more on the broken than the beautiful. Conviction flooded my heart as I realized I was not only good at picking apart God's creation of nature, but I was equally guilty of finding and focusing on what I believed to be my physical flaws. Standing in the mirror, putting my scars under a microscope, I had made them the center of my focus. I now had to retrain my eyes to stop placing my scars in the limelight. I had to learn to stop looking at what I believed to be my physical flaws and open my eyes to the beauty that God has created.

If our flaws are the center of our attention, we will falsely believe they're the center of everyone else's attention. Since the scars were the first thing that I saw when I looked in the mirror, I assumed that everyone else saw them as well. During my middle and high school years, I was so self-conscious about what others thought about my cleft that I would *assume* what others were thinking.

If I saw two people sitting together and laughing and they looked my way, I assumed they were laughing at me. When most teenage girls were flattered, thinking a young man was "checking them out," I assumed he was staring at my cleft lip and palate. Every time someone was looking at me, I immediately attributed it to my deepest insecurity. Rather than conclude they were looking at my outfit, trying to figure out where they recognized me from, or just plain bored and staring off into space, I speculated that they were staring at me because I was born with a cleft lip and palate.

This self-preoccupation, thinking others are talking about us, positively or negatively, is unhealthy in every way. They may have been staring or looking at me for a million reasons. It's not healthy nor fair for me to infer their reasons. While some truly stared at me from time to time, I *magnified* the occurrences in my head as I began to unfairly project my insecurities on others.

I'm not naïve. I'm choosing to believe the best of others, not making assumptions and *allowing God to sort out the rest.* As I have grown, I have realized that most people are too busy thinking and focusing on their own insecurities that they don't have time to focus on mine.

After my new friend Kate told me that she didn't see the scars on my lip, I quickly dismissed her as insane.

"Hey Stacey, do you want to go swimming with us?" Kate asked.

"Oh no, sorry, I can't," I replied.

"You don't know how to swim?" She asked with a confused look on her face.

"No, I can swim. I just can't get water in my ears," I replied.

"Oh; you can wear earplugs," she advised.

I explained, "Yeah, I know but with my cleft lip and palate I have had some horrible ear infections and I don't want to risk another infection."

"With your whaaaat?" She questioned.

This time saying it a little slower, I repeated, "My cleft lip and palate."

"What is that?" She asked again.

"Um…the scars on my face," I answered.

"What scars?" She asked, looking genuinely confused.

I felt I was simply addressing the elephant in the room. But by her response, I actually let the cat out of the bag. She genuinely had no clue what I was talking about. At first, I truly thought she was lying to me. I mean, how could she miss them? However, what I didn't realize was that she truly didn't notice my scars because she was not staring at them as I did. When she spoke to me, she was not staring at the shape of my nose or at the remnants of past incisions. She was looking at me. She saw me as a *whole person*. She was learning about who I was—my interests, likes and dislikes, and she didn't really notice my scars because they did not *represent* me.

Just as she saw me as a whole person, I needed to see myself that way as well. When we take one step back and see the entire picture, we find that every one of us is a miracle of life. By staring at the scars on my face, I was missing the whole picture of how God saw me. Rather than see the eternal, I could only see the temporary. When I took my eyes off of my physical scars, I could see myself for who I really was.

I no longer saw myself as Stacey Verhoff, the girl born with a cleft lip and palate.

I became Stacey Verhoff.

A child of God.

Created anew in Christ Jesus.

Loved unconditionally by God.

Seen and heard by God.

Placed on earth for a time and purpose.

A sister, an aunt, a daughter, coworker and a friend.

Enthusiast of bike rides, athletic events, and meaningful conversations.

Oh, yeah, and one more thing—the scars on my face are from a bilateral cleft lip and palate. Rather than deny that the cleft happened, I acknowledge it as a small part of my story; but it no longer was the *focus*. The scars still have a meaningful part in my journey because God can use my *entire story* for His glory; and I embrace that.

Finding the Good

Just as I always found my scars because I was looking for them, I believe we will find whatever we look for in our lives. If we desire to find the bad, we will find plenty of it. Nevertheless, if we desire to change our perspective and find the good things that God is doing in our lives, we will find plenty of good things as well. Rather than focus on the negative, we should purposefully look for the positives and blessings in our lives and *hold onto that.*

One of my favorite promises in God's Word is that "He causes everything to work together for the good of those who love God and are called according to his purpose."[1] In God's providence, He is working all things for His glory *and* our good. Through the hard times, I can see God's kind hand through the process, all the while working it for my ultimate good.

It is hard to play the victim when we live on the solid foundation of the truth that God first loves us. When we understand that everything that happens to us passes through the hands of God, we realize that while it still isn't easy, we can trust the One who will work it all for our ultimate good. Knowing His very nature is love and His love towards us is everlasting, we can trust the One who journeys through the valley with us. I'm not saying that having a cleft lip and palate is good. I'm saying that in the midst having a cleft, rather than change my situation, God has helped me to see the good that He has brought out of it.

Although I never looked forward to the recovery process, there was one good thing that I eagerly anticipated each time I had surgery. A few days prior, my mom would take me to the grocery store and allow me to pick out my favorite ice cream to eat while my incisions healed. Getting to pick out my own ice cream was a huge deal because growing up, desserts were not a common occurrence in the Verhoff household. Not only was I able to have ice cream, a special treat; but I was also able to *select* my favorite kind and eat it instead of broccoli! It was a truly great experience!

In attempts to avoid "ice cream jealously" that could easily spark a sibling World War III, my mom allowed my siblings to select their own ice cream during this time as well. Frequently, I joked with my brother that I was taking a hit for the team by having the surgery so we could both get ice cream! Even today, my brother admits that he probably looked forward to my surgeries more than he should have because he, too, wanted the treats that came with it.

Ice cream sure was a good thing. However, it's not the only good thing that came in the midst of my cleft lip and palate. While all surgeries can be worrisome, there was something a little extra scary about having surgery on my face. One of my biggest fears was that, if the doctor messed up and made the scars worse, it would be evident for the whole world to see. This fear made the process of selecting a new doctor very difficult when my childhood doctor retired.

After tearing my ACL, some expected me to be nervous for my upcoming surgery. Although I faced separate challenges with rehabilitating my knee afterwards, having a multitude of operations for my cleft lip and palate made an ACL repair seem like nothing. This procedure didn't scare me in the least since this would be my first one that was not on my face. I didn't care how big the scar was on my knee; I was just happy it wouldn't be on my face where everyone could see it! So—although any surgery would be worrisome for most, my prior cleft surgeries prepared me for other types of operations. Again, there was good that came from the multitude of procedures I had faced.

Another blessing in disguise was that, after receiving seven years of speech therapy, this experience gave me an interest in the field of Speech-Language Pathology. Without my own struggles with speech, I wouldn't have been familiar with a profession that I'm now blessed to call my own—and it gave me a passion that leads me in the workplace each day. Through my own experiences, I better understand what it's like to be in the shoes of those I serve. I'm grateful for this perspective.

Do you know the best way to learn how to treat a patient?

By being one yourself.

Although I was required to obtain a degree to become a Speech-Language Pathologist, a degree alone is not adequate to teach me how to treat those I serve. Throughout a multitude of doctor appointments, surgeries, and therapy appointments, I have seen firsthand many medical professionals who genuinely cared for me as a person; and I have experienced a few who treated me more like an issue than someone they desired to help.

While being wheeled into the post-operation recovery room, a nurse's aide approached my bed to assist the nurse. As I was still coming out of the anesthesia, with gauze covering the majority of my face to stop the bleeding, the nurse's aide looked at me and shockingly said, "Oh my! What happened to her face?!?" While she more than likely didn't realize I was alert enough to hear and remember her shocked look and statement, this experience simply reminds me to always treat the individuals I serve as people first, rather than mere problems to be solved or those unworthy of being part of the conversation.

My orthodontist, Dr. Laboe, set the bar high as he genuinely cared for his patients. He was one of my favorites. He always made me feel like I mattered, and he would do whatever necessary to ensure I received the best care. Each appointment, Dr. Laboe greeted me with a smile and worked diligently to make sure my fake teeth fit well and looked as natural as possible. He wanted *me* to feel confident with the pieces he created. Even after moving an hour and half away, Dr. Laboe once made himself available after hours to repair my fake teeth. He willingly fitted me for a new retainer when the old one couldn't be repaired, occasionally not even charging for his services. Throughout my experience with Dr. Laboe, I learned the importance of treating patients like they matter and doing everything within my power to ensure they are well cared for. While I'm far from perfect, my goal is to treat others the same way that so many wonderful professionals have treated me.

Learning to See Beyond Myself

The greatest good that has come from my cleft lip and plate has been the realization that, although my scars tell of my journey with a cleft lip and palate, we all have *scars*. We all have a *story*. Some of our scars are external and visible, while some are internal and unseen. Some share their struggles like an open book while others are a line-by-line read, as they need to develop trust in order to reveal more.

Knowing that we all have scars, rather than hyper-focus on my own scars, I am learning to consider others' scars. In my natural flesh, unless something has touched me firsthand, I'm not overly compassionate. Actually, I'm hardly compassionate. Sometimes my pride and ego take center stage, making me blind to the needs of those around me.

While hiking 2.5-hours up a trail in the Great Smoky Mountains, I could hear my friend breathing hard. Falling many steps behind me, she occasionally stopped to rest and rehydrate. The majority of the hike continued this way, myself in the lead and my friend getting annoyed at my rapid pace up the mountain. Being competitive to a fault, I can't deny that I enjoyed being in the lead. She was exhausted. I wasn't.

Looking back at her standing twenty yards behind me, I quickly became critical. Surely not bold enough to say it aloud, I freely began *hypothesizing* the many reasons for her struggle. "Maybe if she would've exercised a little more or laid off the soda maybe she wouldn't be so tired. If she can't handle this shorter hike, how in the world is she going to handle a *real* hike?!"

About an hour into the trip, as my stomach began to growl, I started dreaming about all the wonderful things my friend had packed for lunch. In a moment, a light bulb *finally* went off in my head. Coming to a sobering moment of correction, I realized "Oh snap! She is exhausted because she has both of our lunches in her backpack, and it's much heavier than mine!"

Secretly hoping this wasn't the case, as it would showcase that

I wasn't a much better athlete, I turned around and headed back toward my friend. Humbly I asked, "Hey, do you want to switch backpacks?" Without hesitation she replied, "Sure!" As we switched backpacks, I immediately noticed that her backpack was significantly heavier than mine. While my backpack totaled 5 pounds, hers was closer to 20 pounds. As we continued the trek, now bearing the heavier load, I quickly grew with exhaustion and was moving at the pace of a tortoise. As I slowed down, my friend became light on her feet and moved ahead with ease like an Olympic athlete on steroids.

Finally arriving at the top of the mountain, I asked, "What do you have in this backpack? It's heavy!" Looking through the bag, I found a First Aid kit, extra water, lunch for the both of us, bug spray, and plenty of technology so that we could record our adventure and have memories for a lifetime. To my embarrassment, I had packed only a can of peaches and some water in my lightweight bag. With my friend willing to carry a heavy load, I was able to eat a nice lunch and have energy for the hike down. I was able to take plenty of pictures and videos, which I still enjoy watching today. Furthermore, if adversity would have struck us on the trail, we could have survived a few days with my friend's supplies. With my measly can of peaches, my stomach would have been growling for the remainder of the hike.

Humbled is how I felt the rest of the day.

It was so easy for me to look at my friend who was struggling with her burdensome backpack and think, "If you would have just done what I did to prepare, this hike wouldn't be so hard." She didn't need my assumptions. She needed me to take the time to *ask what load she was carrying.* Once I learned of the load, she needed me to take my turn carrying the burdensome backpack so we both could get to the top and have an enjoyable hike. I could share all my opinions and thoughts on what she needed to do, but until I took her backpack and started hiking, I had no idea how heavy and burdensome her load truly was.

Sometimes I let my pride and ego take center stage, making it more about me than I should. Sometimes I'm too blinded by my own scars to offer compassion to those hurting around me. *Compassion*, by definition, is having a "deep sympathy and sorrow for another who is stricken by misfortune, accompanied by a strong desire to alleviate the suffering."[2] Compassion literally means "to suffer together."[3] Compassion entails *walking alongside of* someone, rather than trying to obtain a quick "fix" so no one is inconvenienced. It is more than feeling the pain of one who is hurting but it *provokes us to action* to help those suffering.

Our greatest example of compassion is Jesus Christ. Jesus had compassion toward the sick and healed them.[4] He had compassion toward the prodigal son and welcomed him home.[5] *Jesus' compassion led him to action.* He healed the sick and threw a party for the prodigal son. Far greater, His most incomprehensible act of compassion was hanging on the cross for our sins. Our every wayward thought and action, compassionately covered by the blood of Jesus. Wow. How good He is! Compassion is a characteristic of God; and we, too, are called to have compassion.

It's Not All About Me

Even in our darkest times, we can trust that God is with us and will comfort us. The righteous may have many troubles, but the Lord promises to deliver them from those burdens.[6] The Good Shepherd provides comfort and relief for our weary souls, not so we pull inward and isolate ourselves, but so we look outward and offer that same comfort to others.[7]

The Apostle Paul exhorts,

> All praise to God, the Father of our Lord Jesus Christ. God is our merciful Father and the *source of all comfort.* He comforts us in all our troubles so that *we can comfort others.* When they are troubled,

> we will be able to give the same comfort that God
> has given us." (2 Corinthians 1:3-4)

I have long been encouraged by this verse, as it has taught me that no struggle I have ever gone through is wasted. As we overcome our struggles, we can choose to offer our hearts to God and ask him to make us responsive to the *pain of others*.

In Chapter 9, we learned of Ruth's admirable character. Ruth not only demonstrated everyday faithfulness and was a woman of virtuous character, but she also *suffered well with others*. Naomi was not the only one who lost loved ones. Ruth also suffered the loss of her husband and the hope of having an heir. In her own loss, Ruth showed up for Naomi and committed to stay with her.

I cannot imagine Naomi was a barrel of fun while mourning her loss. Naomi not only cried when things were bitter for her before her journey to Bethlehem; but even after they arrived, Naomi told the people to call her *Mara* as the Almighty had made her life very bitter.[8]

During their journey, I'm sure tears flowed.

Probably for both Naomi and Ruth as they mourned *their* losses.

When comforting others, it's easy to feel like we need to have all the answers in order to make a difference. I'm learning that comforting others isn't about having all the answers but choosing to walk with others, even in the midst of our own hurts and struggles.

I would argue that most of our healing does not come when one person claims to have everything figured out; rather, it comes when two hurting people venture towards Christ *together*. When Ruth promised to go with Naomi, she didn't promise that she would know what to do or have a solution or that she would make "everything turnout OK."

Rather, she promised that through it all, she would still be there.

There is something incredibly powerful about a woman who has struggles of her own, yet chooses to walk alongside a sister in Christ. By giving of ourselves to others, we learn that, while our heartaches matter to God, we're not the only ones with struggles. When we continually focus on our own hardships, self-pity consumes us. Not only do we rehearse our own struggles in our minds; but we also magnify the depth of the struggle, leaving us feeling like victims who are powerless in our battle. Being intensely self-absorbed makes it incredibly difficult to look past our own struggles and see that others around us have walked similar roads.

In our moments of pain and discouragement, it's easy to make our wounds the greatest focus. Rather than hand our wounds to Christ, we hold and talk excessively about them, making them our identity. Like a bad habit that is hard to break, the cycle of our wounds continue to come back again, leaving us questioning if we really want to move forward and let them go. While the pain is real, we can move forward by no longer focusing on ourselves and serve a *greater* purpose by helping others.

It isn't that our own struggles are to be ignored or that they don't matter.

They truly do.

While I believe that there are occasional seasons when the struggle may be so intense that we have to step back and allow God to pick up the pieces of our own hearts, we cannot stay in these times long term by making our troubles and issues the focus of our lives. While our struggles do matter to God, when we have spent much time circling around our own insecurities and heartaches, it's healthy to take our eyes off of ourselves and be reminded that *this life isn't all about us.* It is then that we see God's heart for His most prized possession: people. Our main objective is to no longer focus on what we are not or what we believe we lack. Our primary focus becomes living for what really matters: sharing the hope of Jesus Christ and helping others grow into the fullness God desires.

By turning our focus on others around us, we take the focus off of ourselves and what we think our life should look like; and we learn to *embrace the life we have been given.* In learning this, we loosen our grip on this life and let it go for the cause of Christ. We lose ourselves and *we find Him.*

In the search to receive healing from the emotional challenges of being born with a cleft lip and palate, I have come to realize that it was never about my cleft. When I focus on my cleft, I focus on *myself.* Although I'm still a work in progress and I'm still extremely selfish more than I care to admit, I want to grow to be more about my Father's business than my own.

CHAPTER 11

Cultivating Joy

"What is the deepest root of your joy: What God gives to you? Or what God is for you?"

-John Piper

Although I didn't mind getting the day off school, having to spend my time at the doctor's office wasn't my definition of fun. Whenever I had an appointment, the day was long, tiring, and boring. Not having specialists in our hometown, my mom sometimes drove over two hours to take me to the doctor. Although it requires no physical effort, spending a significant portion of the day riding in a car is sometimes tiresome.

Arriving early to the appointment, I sat in the waiting room longer than expected. When I was called back, my excitement was short-lived when I realized there were still three other patients to be seen ahead of me. The nurse took my vitals and charted my updated medical history, and then there was more ... waiting. Finally, the doctor arrived. I returned for many follow-up appointments that seemed to take the same trend: like they were never going to end. I wished at the time that I were spending my time elsewhere; however, I knew these appointments were necessary.

Although they were best for me, being joyful while going to medical appointments wasn't natural for me. Sometimes being joyful is easy. Joy comes easily when our circumstances are good, right? We're joyful when we get the big job promotion. We're joyful when we graduate high school or when we arrive at our long-anticipated wedding day. However, true joy isn't dependent on good circumstances. True joy is choosing to rejoice at all times, even when our situations are unfavorable.

Although finding and choosing joy in difficult situations is not typically automatic, it's possible. And though she probably never realized it, my mom taught me the fine art of having fun and cultivating joy in the midst of mundane situations. She was not perfect, but she was intentional about not allowing stresses and frustrations to ruin her day.

Although my mom expected us to all pitch in to clean the house, her rules were simple: as long as we completed our chores in a timely manner, we were encouraged to have fun while doing them. We had to sweep the floor, but there were no rules against cranking up the music and using the broom as an air guitar once the floor was clean. After mopping, we were free to slide across it with our socks on. Even while doing mundane tasks like washing and drying dishes, we could grab a cup, turn it upside down, and use it as a microphone to sing along as long as we made sure to put it in the right cupboard when we were finished. For my mom, productivity and fun went hand in hand. Whether it be daily household chores or doctor appointments, her motto was simple: Why choose to be miserable just because something isn't naturally enjoyable? Instead, *make* it fun.

While traveling to a doctor's appointment, picking up a sweet treat was a must. While my mom and I are different in many ways, we could easily agree on one thing: A delicious treat always comes in the form of...chocolate! Twix Bars. M&Ms. Hershey Kisses. Milky Ways. Butterfinger. It honestly did not matter. We were not picky! As long as it had a solid layer of chocolate!

During one of our adventures, my mom purchased a bag of plain M&Ms for us to share. It was a hot summer day. I rolled my window down to feel the breeze while driving through town. As my mom stopped at a red light, anticipating the fresh chocolate aroma, I eagerly attempted to open the bag so we could dig in! Struggling to open, I began forcefully prying. With one big effortful pull, the bag exploded open and the majority of the M&Ms flew out the window and the rest on the floor of the car. While I was initially shocked, uncontained laughter followed as we drove away leaving a trail of candy as if it were a parade!

We may have shared many mundane doctor appointments, but we shared many more laughs. My mom helped to create memories that will last a lifetime and taught me to find joy in the simple things in life.

Simple things.

Like M&Ms for the long car ride.

Throughout many years of doctor and therapy appointments, my mom did her absolute best to find joy in the process. She desired to walk out the routine events of life, the things that were easy and the things that were difficult, with a joyful heart.

Running Ragged

After moving out of my parents' home, I took over the scheduling and coordinating of my remaining medical appointments. Desiring a second set of ears to hear what the doctor had to say, I asked my mom to meet me at the doctor's office near Detroit, Michigan. With my mom coming from Northwest Ohio and me coming from the opposite side of Michigan, we each had a two-hour drive. Greeting each other in the parking lot, we walked together into the office, only to find that we had gone to the wrong doctor!

My appointment that day was with another doctor, which was forty-five minutes from where we stood. The secretary reluctantly informed me that there was no way we could make the drive before their office closed. This was my first time scheduling my own appointment, and I messed it up! Agitated and annoyed at my mistake, I irritably turned toward my mom. Rather than join my frustration, she smiled and said, "Well, where do you want to go eat?" Eat?! I wasted my time and her time—and now I had to take another day off work to reschedule my doctor's appointment! I was too upset to think about eating!

In her wisdom, my mom encouraged me to not let it ruin my day but rather go eat since it was already past lunchtime. After eating, relaxing, and conversing with my mom, I began to realize it was far from a wasted trip. With food in my stomach and a little rest, I could now see that the situation was not the end of the world and certainly not worth the frustration that I had given it.

Elijah, one of God's prophets, was no stranger to discouragement. Elijah became highly discouraged when threatened by Queen Jezebel because of his faithfulness to the Lord. Afraid for his own life and exhausted from traveling, Elijah sat down under a tree and prayed that he might die. In anguish, Elijah pleaded, "I have had enough Lord. Take my life, for I am no better than my ancestors who have already died."[1]

Greatly discouraged, Elijah was ready to throw in the towel.

We have all been there—overwhelmed by life and feeling like we can no longer stand. So, what is God's response to His depressed, hungry, tired, and discouraged servant? As he was sleeping, an angel of the Lord woke him up and told him to *get something to eat and drink*. Apparently, the angel of the Lord knew what it meant to be "hangry" before we termed the phrase!

After resting and eating, the food strengthened him for the journey to Mount Sinai. Truly, eating and resting are gifts of renewal, which allow us to see more clearly. Although it can be a challenge, we don't need to wait for life to calm down before we rest. Just as Jesus took a nap while on the boat in the midst of a storm, we, too, can rest and nap during the stormy situations of our lives, trusting the One who can calm every storm. When discouragement steals our joy, we do well to remember God's call to eat and rest.

Finding Joy in the Unknown

It was the afternoon before my final surgery. My mom and I started the trek to our hotel, which was located within a few miles from the hospital. We had chosen to leave the day before and spend the night closer to the hospital, as the scheduled surgery was very early the next morning. My dad would join us after getting off of work. After arriving at the hotel, we decided to go out to eat for one more meal before I had to fast for the upcoming surgery. Selecting a restaurant that I had never been to before, we had a good time. The food was great. We had fun watching sporting events and sharing good conversation. After we finished eating and gathered our belongings to leave, a sense of reality overcame me.

I was not there to eat a nice meal and watch sporting events. I was there to have surgery in the morning. Soon, the fun-filled and carefree mood of devouring good food left, and tension filled my heart. Honestly, surgeries always made me feel uneasy. Yet, in the midst of this familiar uneasiness, this evening was a little different. A small portion of joy filled the air, knowing that this was *finally* my last major surgery.

The next morning we awoke before dawn and traveled the few short miles to the hospital. After registering, I quickly found myself in the pre-op room where the nurse, phlebotomist, and anesthesiologist completed their pre-surgery tests and questionnaires. Initially, everything was moving very quickly; and then—it came time to wait for the doctor.

We waited.

And we *waited*.

After what seemed like forever, the doctor and his nurse came into the room and informed my parents and me that he had to cancel my surgery. Up until this day, I had countless surgeries, and none had been canceled. The doctor explained that after checking my blood work, they found my platelets were too low for surgery. He explained that platelets were responsible to clot my blood, and I would require an adequate number of platelets to control and stop the bleeding during surgery. Without the appropriate platelet count, I was at a high risk of bleeding excessively and losing too much blood. He informed me that I should schedule an appointment with an oncologist to figure out why my platelets were low and how we should proceed.

The drive home was quiet. I guess we were all trying to figure out what had happened. I had "low …" what did he call those things again?

Platelets?

I had never heard of such a thing.

Weird. Why were they low all of a sudden? This wasn't my first surgery rodeo.

Since we were at the hospital so early that morning, after our two-hour drive back home, there was still plenty of time left in the day. It was only 11 am, and I had no plans. After all, I was supposed to be recovering from surgery today. Sitting at the kitchen table, I turned on the laptop and began doing my "research" to find out what could be wrong with me. Remember; this was at a time when the dinosaurs roamed the earth and I was not able to simply ask, "Alexa, what are causes of low platelets?" So, pulling up Google, I typed my question into the search engine and within seconds, I had my list of possible "diagnoses." The list ranged from *Don't worry it's just a fluke* to *You have Leukemia and will be dead in one minute.*

Wonderful.

Fear of the unknown gripped me. Spinning my wheels over what was wrong, I knew Googling a diagnosis was not a good idea, but I grasped at anything to gain an answer…even if it was wrong. While my mind was whirling, my mom peacefully looked at me and said,

"Why don't you go hangout with Makayla today and just wait for answers until we go see the oncologist?"

Although she appeared calm on the external, I knew she was shaken up on the inside as much as I was. However, she was choosing something different from the fear that was within her. She was choosing *joy* today, over worrying about our unknown of tomorrow. She was choosing not to let the fear of the unknown steal the present day.

She encouraged me to hang out with my friend—and for me, as well, to choose to enjoy today over circling and spinning around my fears for tomorrow. I didn't have a diagnosis from a doctor, but I had choices. I could sulk. Whine. Throw a pity party. Honestly, option three sounded good. I don't mind a good self-indulging pity party as long as there is cake and ice cream involved. I had many choices. I could sit with Google and dream up horrific outcomes; or I could enjoy today with my best friend from high school.

I'm glad my mom helped me choose the latter. As always, Makayla and I enjoyed some good laughs—not because life was roses and rainbows and I knew how everything would turn out. Not because I was a stellar person who had all the answers. But because I was learning to *choose joy*. I was learning to choose today over tomorrow. I was learning *intentional* joy.

Finding Joy in the Moment

I am still learning to choose joy. Personally, my most frequent cause of being overwhelmed isn't when I'm dealing with the issues that are at hand today but when I entertain my fears for tomorrow. Often I fail to pray and hand my concerns over to God. Instead, I wonder, "How am *I* going to do all this?" I take control of my life, leaving me joyless and full of fear. In my isolation, I falsely believe that it's all up to me to make all things right rather than asking, "God, how are *You* going to walk me through this?"

At heart, I'm a country girl. I like the peace and calm of country living. I love a good sunset fading over the cornfield. I enjoy watching the farmers plant crops during the long summer days. Country living has its own beautiful scenery. Having your own space is amazing. However, being single, I don't want to live in the boondocks by myself. The house I live in seems like it was made for me. It's in a subdivision, with great neighbors on both sides of me; I feel I'm not alone. An additional benefit? The backyard butts right up to a field with picture-worthy sunsets practically each night.

Four years ago, I bought this house. It felt as if God handpicked it for me. The entire process of house hunting was long and stressful. I put a few solid offers on other houses. They fell through. I was disappointed and confused. Then unexpectedly, this house opened up for me. I placed the offer, and they accepted. It seemed so easy— as if God said, "Here; *this* house is for you."

Although I know God led me here so I could enjoy the scenery and security, I have to be honest that most times when I look at the cornfield, awe and wonder do not fill my heart. Mainly the fear of tomorrow fills my heart. What if they sell the field and someone builds a house right behind me? What if my neighborhood becomes unsafe? What if? What if?

Sometimes, I exhaust myself with the "what ifs" of tomorrow. But slowly, I'm learning joy in the moment. Tonight I enjoyed a sunset. No worrying about tomorrow. Well, maybe a little.

Sigh.

I'm still a work in progress. Yet, I know I'm not alone. Living in the joy of the moment is challenging for most of us. Although I'm not a parent, through engaging in meaningful conversations with those who are, I've learned that finding joy in the present moment when raising children can be a challenge. Parents can easily miss the moments of joy of the child right in front of them when they're too busy worrying about the future. While it's easy to worry about the future of any child, the fear of the unknown may be intensified when the child is born with a birth defect.

With the multitude of surgeries and specialist referrals, it can be overwhelming for parents of children with additional needs. The weight of "Am I doing enough for my child?" and "Am I doing the right thing?" can be burdensome. These parents may worry about which surgeon to entrust to their child; they may stress about learning new ways to help their children progress in their speech and language development. They might lose sleep with the added stresses that keep their brains constantly highlighting the never-ending to-do lists. And on top of the mental struggles, these parents likely are met with added physical exhaustion from the everyday hustle and bustle of getting their children to all of the scheduled appointments.

While conversing with my brother at a wedding, a little guy around three years of age, who was born with a cleft lip and palate, sprinted pass us with a huge mischievous smile on his face. He ran with pure freedom, running to his heart's content. My brother, a new father himself, looked at me and said, "Look how incredibly happy that little guy is. You can't miss *this moment*."

I couldn't agree more.

Often our concerns and fears for tomorrow make us miss the joy of a child right in front of us. Do our worries for tomorrow blind us to the *blessing* of a child that God has given us? Are we worrying about our child's teenage and adult years and missing the happy and energetic three-year-old who's looking at us for attention right here, right now?

In order to be joyful, we do not have to bury our heads in the sand and act as if problems do not exist. There are problems. Sleepless nights. Scheduling conflicts. Genuine concern for our children's welfare. We have real problems that need real solutions.

I am not saying that we should ignore the future. I'm saying that there is a difference between *planning* and *worrying*. Planning is a good thing, which helps us make responsible choices today. We should plan for tomorrow. We need to schedule appointments, and we need to research reputable doctors and therapists for our children.

In planning, we look ahead to real problems and do what we can today. We then rest in the arms of Jesus as He holds our future secure. We can confidently entrust to Him our unknown future.

Worrying is when we choose to look ahead and fabricate situations that may or may not happen. In fact, very little of what we ever worry about actually will come to fruition. Unlike planning for what will likely happen (i.e. I will retire someday), worrying often creates a *slippery slope* in which we irrationally envision the most extreme failure (i.e. I will retire and have no money, no friends, no shelter, and eat grass to survive). While the extremes we take our worries to can be comical in hindsight, in the moment our fears can seem extremely real and plausible.

I don't mean to brag, but I'm really good at allowing irrational fears about tomorrow to steal my joy for today. I frequently find myself jumping aboard the irrational-fear train and riding it over the cliff of despair. Only as the train plummets to the ground and is about to explode do I finally awaken from my created fantasy world of make-believe fears. Coming desperately back to God, I ask Him to reign my thoughts back upon what is true and worthy of praise.

When overwhelmed with tomorrow, we need to honestly answer the question, "Am I planning, or am I worrying?" You may be a great planner, but you may be an even better worrier. When burdened by our tomorrow, we have a choice to allow fear and worry to magnify our problems. In the midst of challenging circumstances, we must ask ourselves if we're seeing this situation as an opportunity for God to build our faith and magnify Him in our lives or whether we're feeding and enlarging our fears. Joy and peace come when we choose to trust God instead of what we see and feel in any given moment.[2] Rather than building our lives on fear, we must build our lives on learning to trust God in all things.

Anchoring into Joy

As much laughter that it brought, true and anchored joy is not found in M&M parades on a hot summer day. As much fun as we had, true and anchored joy is not found in the form of laughter with your best friend. The lasting fullness of joy is only found in the presence of God.[3] Even in the most challenging situations, in Christ there is always true joy.

I can always rejoice because, for me, Jesus Christ endured the cross and granted me eternal salvation in Him.[4] Knowing He is the Rock of our salvation, we can shout joyfully.[5] We can celebrate with joy that our peace comes through Jesus, and we are now called friends of God. We experience joy when we obey His laws and search for Him with all of our hearts. [6]

True joy is found when we lift up our eyes, taking them off of our problems and see Christ Jesus as our *all in all.* Joy is found when we magnify Christ more than we magnify our problems. As we abide, walk, and fellowship in Christ and the Holy Spirit, we bear the fruit of true joy.[7] After all, the joy of the Lord is our strength.[8]

There is no one better to learn the art of intentional joy from than the Apostle Paul. Paul suffered. He was imprisoned, stoned, and beaten. He experienced shipwreck. Yet, Paul chose the joy of the Lord. Even in the midst of trials, Paul exhorted, "Always be full of joy in the Lord!"[9] Joy comes when we stop worrying and choose instead to pray about everything. Joy comes when we choose to thank God for all He has already done.[10]

Today and every day, we have a choice. A choice to let joy or fear take center stage of our day. Today and every day, we will actively choose what will lead us through our day. I falter and fail more than I care to admit, but with the Holy Spirit's help, I want to choose joy.

CHAPTER 12

Finding Malta

"Peace I leave with you. My peace I give to you...
Do not let your heart be troubled."

-John 14:27 (NIV)

"Come to me, all you who are weary and burdened,
and I will give you rest."

-Matthew 11:28 (NIV)

Throughout many team-bonding experiences, I had one too many opportunities to participate in the infamous "Trust Fall." You know, the one where you would stand on a platform with your back to a group of teammates who had arms extended, knees bent, ready to embrace your entire body weight as you plummeted to the earth below? One by one, each team member would take her turn building trust in her teammates as she blindly freefell into their arms. I dreaded this team-bonding experience. I struggled trusting that my teammates would catch me. I struggled believing that my peers would be strong enough to stop my momentum and prevent me from being injured.

Trusting is hard. It requires a sense of vulnerability and reliance on someone else. In this instance, it required that I let go and let someone else carry my weight. Each year I completed the trust fall, no matter how nervous I was, they always caught me when I fell. Soon, with each fall and catch, I learned to trust. On a larger scale, with each faithful act of Lord, I am learning to trust Him in all things. Learning to trust Him has been an ongoing process, as I tend to create the illusion of control in my life.

What helped shatter this illusion, though, was something that I feared even a bit more than trust-building exercises: rollercoasters. Although I'm not a rollercoaster enthusiast, my friend Kim is. For her, the faster, the better. Although I was nervous about going on this ride, being competitive in nature, I was surely not going to admit that I was afraid. She would never let me live it down. So here, I found myself standing in a very long line on an extremely hot summer day, waiting for a ride I never wanted to go on in the first place. Although I prayed the rapture would occur before it was our turn, we unfortunately made our way to the front and boarded the coaster.

As the rollercoaster operator eagerly announced that we would be ascending and then dropping 400 feet while going over 120 mph, Kim's eyes lit up with joy and eager anticipation. Being sure this ride would be my demise, I turned ghostly white. Although the operator described this *amazing* coaster with great excitement, I could only envision this *amazing* coaster flying off the track and crashing to the ground.

As I was still looking for an escape route, the operator pulled down my harness to secure me on the ride. Knowing there was no turning back, I pulled the harness as tight as possible, sucking in every ounce of fat in my midsection and limiting my ability to breathe.

Ready. Set. Go.

We took off sooooo fast!

My heart leaping through my chest, I gripped the two small

metal handles attached to my harness with white-knuckled force. As we flew around the track at an unimaginable speed, Kim was screaming with excitement. She exclaimed, "Look at the birds!"

Birds?!

I couldn't see any birds. My eyes had been clamped shut from the very moment we took off!

Hearing the laughter of my friend as she threw her hands in the air and enjoyed the rollercoaster at its full capacity, I suddenly questioned myself: "Stacey, what are you doing? You're gripping this bar as if you could actually hang on if your harness did break." Here I was, on a fierce roller coaster falsely believing I was the one in control. Gripping two tiny metal handlebars, I falsely believed that if my harness broke, I was physically strong enough to hang on as it twisted and turned at over 120 mph.

The reality was, no matter how much I failed to enjoy the ride by shutting my eyes and clinging on, in my own strength I was not in any control on this rollercoaster ride. Realizing my lack of control, I slowly opened my eyes and saw the delight on my friend's face. Watching her throw her hands in the air and looking incredibly weightless, I released my grip and slowly lifted my hands in surrender. As we propelled along the track, I no longer felt fear, but a sense of wonder that this powerful piece of equipment was doing all the work and my only job was to *let go* and *enjoy the ride.*

Trusting God sometimes feels like a rollercoaster ride. In my best moments, my hands are fully surrendered as I let God have complete control. Yet, in my worst moments, I find myself with a death grip to gain even an ounce of control, as I fear that God isn't adequate to meet my needs. More often than not, I rely on my own strength instead of His. Ripping the reigns from God's hands, I take the lead in attempts to control my situation. I take on an extra job so that I have greater security in my bank account; and I overcommit myself to obligations, simply assuring others still need me. Then, utterly exhausted and depleted of any energy, I become irritable with God because of the "road He has given me." Yet, in His gentle kindness, He reminds me that *He* has not given me this road. *I have created this situation myself* as I grasp for self-reliance and control, rather than trusting Him. Then He reminds me I'm free to lay it down any time I choose.

Other times in our lives, the road we're on is difficult with no choice of our own. One of the most challenging aspects of having a cleft lip and plate is the financial strain that it can place upon families. While raising their four children, my parents did not have a lot of money. My dad worked a blue-collar job; and although we had everything we needed, there was not extra money for cushion. During a season of their early marriage, my parents had only one car and eventually were gifted a second car that cost $50. Without extra financial security and incoming medical bills, my parents received a crash course in "Trusting God 101."

With the many surgeries and dental work that my brother and I required, my parents were no strangers to payment plans. It seemed like, once they paid off one medical bill, there was another one in the mailbox. As we grew older, my parents joked they had a lot of money in our teeth and we had better smile to show them off! When picking on my mom, she joked that we had better be nice or she will stop making payments and the bank will come and repossess us! It was all clean fun. We knew our parents would move mountains to ensure we had all the surgeries we needed. However, no matter how much they made light of the situation, the cost of the medical expenses was a sobering reality.

Each insurance company is different. Some companies pay for cleft repair without any issues. Our insurance company initially denied payment for a few surgeries. They incorrectly deemed the repair *cosmetic and optional* rather than reconstructive and medically necessary. With my dad working long hours to provide for our family, my mom spent many days on the phone with the insurance company. With each phone call, she tried to explain that it was their responsibility to pay their portion of the upcoming surgery, as it was a reconstruction of a birth defect. This whole process caused much pressure and stress for my parents, as they didn't have the extra money to cover the whole cost of the surgeries.

Admittedly, it was not one of her finest moments. After spending over six months calling the insurance company to explain that this surgery was not cosmetic, my mom was at her wits end. Being transferred to many different people and getting nowhere, my mom blurted out, "I never wish anyone to have a child with a cleft lip and palate; but I now wish that you would know someone who has one so that you would finally understand that this is NOT cosmetic!"

The stress and financial burden of medical bills are real, as the necessary procedures can be very costly. Even when the insurance companies do pay their portion, families have financial obligations of their own. Although the stress was very heavy at times, with the surgeries behind them and nearing retirement, my parents can now look back and see that *God always provided for their every need.* Even when they didn't know from where the money would come, God was seeing them through.

At times throughout our journey, God reminds us of His faithful love and provision. After over twenty years of making payment plans for the services needed for my cleft lip and palate, my parents scheduled my last major dental procedure. While selecting the date of the procedure, the office manager informed my parents that the insurance company would only cover a very small portion of the cost. They would be responsible for the full payment. In order to move ahead and schedule, they would need to provide $10,000 to cover the cost of the dental implants.

Moving forward, my parents took out a loan for thousands of dollars, not being certain if they would get any of the money back. After three months of waiting for the final verdict on who was going to pay the bill, the biller sent a notice that the insurance company paid the bill in *full.* This was jaw-dropping, celebration-required news for my parents. Not only were my parents dumbfounded by the payment, but the office manager was *stunned* as well. She was certain the insurance company wouldn't cover the procedure. Even the doctor said he had never seen an insurance company pay the full amount for that procedure in his many years as a prosthodontist.

After all those years of my parents calling insurance companies and making payments for surgeries and orthodontic work, God orchestrating the full payment was a reminder of His faithfulness. Feeling His warm embrace, God dropped the gavel on the question of, "God, are you trustworthy to provide?"

Boom!

Yes, He is trustworthy! He is faithful!

Stamping our final bill *paid in full*, God reminded us that He is our provider and He provides *so well*. Though my parents had financial concerns, God promised to supply all of our needs, according to His glorious riches.[1] He surely is Jehovah-Jireh the one who sees our needs and provides.

Great Trust to Great Discouragement

When I recall God's faithfulness in my life, I can't help but be filled with faith, knowing He will provide. In these moments, I truly believe He is trustworthy in providing for my needs. Yet, sometimes I forget and begin to doubt that He holds my future secure. Even after witnessing God's faithfulness in my parents' finances while raising *two* children with cleft lip and palates, I have to admit, I still struggle to trust God in all things.

Although I cannot say that I have ever asked God for a miracle of the same proportion, I can easily relate to Elijah, the man *full of faith and at times full of discouragement*. In the previous chapter, we found Elijah greatly discouraged and laying under a tree, wishing to die. But Elijah wasn't always discouraged and running in fear. No. Like you and me, he had finer moments as well. Reading more about Elijah, I'm amazed at what God's servant had done just before he lay under the fig tree in despair.

Shortly before becoming so discouraged, with great faith,

Elijah challenged Baal's prophets on Mount Carmel to a contest to demonstrate the identity of the One True God. To no avail, the prophets of Baal called on their god to set fire to the wood alter, while Elijah boldly and powerfully called upon God to prove He was God of Israel.[2]

Not only did Elijah believe that God would reveal himself, but he drenched the wood with water three times, so much that water ran around the alter and even filled the trench.[3] After Elijah called, the fire of the Lord flashed down from heaven and burned up the young bull, the wood, the stones, and the dust. The fire even licked up the water from the trench! Seeing this, all the people fell face down on the ground and cried out, "The Lord—he is God!"[4]

Elijah, so full of faith and trust that God was who He said He was, called upon the Lord to perform a miracle of miracles to show Himself to His people.

Wow, what faith!

Yet almost immediately after this experience, Elijah wished to die.

Going from faith to discouragement so quickly, I too can relate. There are times I truly believe that God has it all under His control—times when it just seems so easy to trust God, knowing that He holds the situation in the palm of His hand. When things are good, when things go as I hoped and planned, it's easy for me to trust and declare my faith in God. Yet, in the moments when I do not understand what God is doing, in the moments when life hurts, it's easy to quickly fall into a place of discouragement. From faith that God can do anything, to questioning if He even cares, I too can relate to Elijah.

In our moments of questioning and doubt, there is good news: God did not define Elijah by his moments of discouragement. Instead, He provided for his physical needs and sent an angel to strengthen him for the rest of the journey. We, too, should not define ourselves by the moments we're overwhelmed and discouraged. These moments of discouragement are opportunities to halt on the path of fear and worry and agree to be led back to our Rock, the One who knows the beginning from the end.

Turning 180 degrees from worry and fear, facing God, we find the complete opposite of worry as we learn to trust Him. Putting aside our concerns, we lay our lives and our children's lives into the hands of God; and we say, "God, I trust you. I may not know what you're doing, but I trust you." We may trust God with the next 50 years, the next year, or maybe just the next day; but we're learning to *trust*. In trusting in Him, we come to a place our weary hearts ache for: rest in His arms. Fear and hopelessness vanish. Peace, confidence, and assuredness become our banner.

While I have not yet achieved giving complete trust in every area of my life to Christ, He is teaching me moment by moment. Trust isn't that I never fear or worry. Trust is making a daily choice to refocus on God when I have given the cares of this life greater attention than to Him. After trying to manufacture all on my own, trust is when I realize I have picked up my own burden and need to return it at His feet. God does not define us by the moments we're overwhelmed; rather, He invites us to lay it all back down at His feet and rest in Him.

Finding Malta

Driving on desolate highways in Idaho, my friend Aubrie slept in the passenger seat. She was recovering from driving the last four hours of our trip. With the sun shining and my favorite music on the radio, I hadn't a care in the world. With a quarter tank of gas left, I needed to stop at the next gas station. As I continued to drive, the area became more rural, and all the signs of life that I had seen were miles and miles in the rearview mirror.

Not phased with the change in scenery, I continued driving, thinking that we were just in the countryside and would be shortly coming upon a town with life once again.

I drove and drove.

And drove and drove.

Still no sign of life.

Starting to become a little uneasy as the gas tank was nearing an eighth of a tank, I woke Aubrie up from her peaceful sleep.

"Hey, wake up!" I nudged her forcefully.

"Wake up! We're almost out of gas. We have less than thirty miles until empty, and I haven't seen any sign of life for miles!"

Finally coming out of her slumber and being the more level-headed one, Aubrie grabbed her phone and searched for the nearest gas station.

"Just stay on this road, and there is a gas station five miles ahead."

With a sense of relief, I continued driving until we saw a bright orange sign in the distance. Squinting my eyes to see, the sign read, "Highway closed. Detour left."

"Highway closed?! Are we going to have enough gas to follow the crazy detour?!"

Unbothered and getting slightly annoyed, she replied, "Yes! Just take the detour!"

Taking the detour, the paved road quickly transitioned to a dirt road. Suddenly, we came upon a wooden sign staked in the ground that read, "Gas Ahead. One mile."

"Oh thank God!" With hope in sight, my nerves finally began to calm.

As we neared the one-mile mark, bringing the car to a snail's pace, our eyes beheld an old beat-down, dilapidated building that apparently at one time, a *long* time ago, was a gas station. Feeling the rumbling of the emotional volcano that was about to explode within me, I did everything I could to keep my fear and frustration in check!

"What are we going to do? If we run out of gas, there are no humans in this part of the world to help us!"

Again, being the voice of reason and reassuring me of her plan,

Aubrie showed me the map of the actual gas station she had located in a small town nearby.

"Calm down Stacey. Take this turn and this road will take us to town. There is a gas station there."

Not wanting to get my hopes up, I waited to celebrate until I saw that this gas station did not resemble the days of John Wayne. Running on what I assumed were fumes, we drove a few more miles, and around 3 pm, we entered a small town called Malta, Idaho. A sign on the door read that the gas station closed at 5:30 pm on the weekdays and was closed all day on Sundays. Never in my life was I more excited for it to be a Monday.

Aubrie and I still laugh about our Malta, Idaho experience to this day. As Paul found refuge on the Island of Malta after being shipwrecked,[5] we found refuge in a different Malta when looking for gasoline.

Malta.

Some argue it means "a place of refuge."

After my Malta experience, I agree.

Although the small town of Malta served as a refuge when we were running out of gas, there is a strong refuge we can always trust. Regardless if we're in the Middle-of-Nowhere Idaho or doing day-to-day life and trying to figure out how we will pay for surgeries or dental work, the Lord is our refuge and fortress, the One in whom we can trust.[6]

God is our refuge in which we can give our burdens and find rest for our weary souls.[7] We see the birds, who do not plant, harvest, or store food in barns, yet our Heavenly Father feeds them. Aren't we far more valuable to God? If God cares so wonderfully for them, will He not certainly care for us?[8] In the midst of stressful situations, our Malta is always there. Drawing us back into His loving arms, God reminds us to seek His Kingdom above anything else; and He promises to give us everything we need.[9] Our Refuge teaches us that we will keep in perfect peace when we trust and fix our thoughts on Him.[10]

When grounded in the truth that the Lord loves us immeasurably, we learn that we can trust Him in all things. Knowing He loves me, I can trust my cleft journey to Him, understanding that *He will see me through.* The same God who shut the mouth of a lion can surely provide financially for surgeries for a cleft lip and palate. The same God, who split the sea for Moses, sees and cares for our needs as well.

In remembering this, we find our Malta. *We find our rest in Him.*

CHAPTER 13

It's Not Your Fault

"Don't shine so others can see you. Shine so that through you others can see Him."

-C.S. Lewis

"I believe in Christ like I believe in the sun. Not because I can see it, but by it, I can see everything else."

-C.S. Lewis

Throughout this book, I have written from the perspective of my own personal struggles. However, I would be amiss to fail to mention that a cleft lip and palate is not only difficult for the individual experiencing it—but it can also be extremely challenging for the parents, especially mothers. Although as a child I was completely oblivious to my parents' trials, after becoming an adult, we have shared many wonderful conversations to better understand one another's journey. So, in this last chapter of my story, I will start from a different perspective—the struggles of my parents.

With her list in hand, my mom walked the aisles at the local grocery store. She hadn't planned to stop at the store but needed a few essential items. I was a newborn, a few days old, laying in my carrier with the receiving blanket draped over top.

Briefly turning her back to me, my mom reached for an item on the top shelf. As she reached up, an acquaintance of hers happened to pass by. Occasionally crossing paths with one another while running errands, she had seen my mom's baby belly growing the past nine months. Excited to see that her baby was finally here, she exclaimed, "You had your baby!" Quickly pulling back the blanket to admire the newborn, the woman gasped as she saw the gaping opening in my lip and the roof of my mouth.

To no fault of her own, seeing my unrepaired cleft lip and palate caught the woman off guard. This occurred before society freely posted pictures of children with unrepaired cleft lip and palates. I was born in the mid-80s, a time when images of children with cleft lip and palate were not just a simple Google search or online fundraiser away. This woman was surprised. She never heard of or saw a cleft lip and palate. I don't share this story to shame the woman; it wasn't her fault. I share it to help us understand the challenges that some mothers face—not just only with the child's immediate circumstances but also from external perceptions.

My mom experienced other awkward and painful moments as well. In the 80s, when giving birth to a child, it was not uncommon to have a semi-private room at the hospital. The room was a single room that two mothers and their babies shared. The rooms were small, so it was inevitable that when guests would come to visit the other mother and baby, they would pass by the other room occupants. Often met with awkward glances, the visitors would usually turn away from my mom or other relatives to avoid eye contact, as they were unsure what to say or do.

My mom wanted her baby to be adored and snuggled just like the rest. It must have hurt to watch others so smitten over the babies without birth defects—wanting to cuddle or hold them...singing their praises. But my mom felt the cold disconnection—people turning away from her baby because they just weren't sure what to say. I'm sure in those moments, she just wanted others to see the gold that she saw in her child.

My mom wasn't the only one who struggled with other's reactions. I have heard other women share similar stories. Recently, a new mom of a child who had just finished his first major surgery, openly shared her frustrations about others' reactions to her baby. She confided that before her son's surgeries, others asked many questions about his cleft lip and palate. Questions like when he would get it repaired or how the doctor appointments were going.

Only after he completed the surgeries did people start asking seemingly "normal" questions about her child—questions about what he liked, how he slept, how old he was. This young mom wished that others would have asked questions about *him* all along— not just about his cleft lip and palate. The questions about the cleft lip and palate didn't bother her; she just wanted others to see that there was more to her son than his anomaly.

For my parents and many others, not only are there struggles before the initial surgery is complete, but there are challenges as their child ages. Parents become overwhelmed when they have to physically restrain a young child when nurses and doctors perform medical procedures. The heartache is real as the parents hold their child down for his or her own good; yet the confused child looks back at the parent wondering, "Why aren't you protecting me? Why are you helping them hurt me?"

It can overwhelm a parent to hand his or her infant to a surgeon. Consoling an upset and irritable baby the first night after surgery can overwhelm any heart. Limiting the baby's activity and placing socks over her hands so she doesn't pick at the stitches is a challenge. A new mother of a child with a cleft lip and palate may feel alone as she navigates the unfamiliar challenge of trying to feed her infant who doesn't have adequate lip and palate closure. It breaks a heart to see her baby struggling to suck on a bottle or lose milk out of the mouth or through the nose. The appropriate concern that her child is getting adequate nutrition is overwhelming.

The struggle is real. As the child ages, playtime also becomes a source of stress and great concern for the parents of a child with cleft lip and palate or other anomaly. Any mother longs desperately to keep her child safe—praying no one would hurt her child. And with an anomaly, those concerns are heightened. What should be a fun occasion is riddled with fear from the new mother, who often will be concerned that others will stare or poke fun at her child because of his or her differences. The mother's fears are met either with validation when her child is picked on or great relief when her child is socially accepted without question of the facial deformity.

Since learning more from my parents' perspective, I now understand we *all* had struggles to overcome...and this wasn't my battle alone. Although the cleft lip and palate brought my own unique internal battles, there was one additional challenge my mom faced that I had never experienced—the internal conflict of *guilt*.

The Weight of Guilt

When moving to a new town, my mom had the common concerns of enrolling her children in an unfamiliar school district. Would the school provide a quality education? Would her children make new friends? In addition to those concerns, my mom couldn't help but be concerned that the kids might pick on my brother and me because of our cleft lip and palates. As we walked toward the soccer field for my first practice with my new team, I innocently felt the eager anticipation of looking forward to playing a game I loved, while my mom felt the uneasiness of the fear that a child may make a comment towards me that would deflate my joyful childlike spirit.

I have an amazing mother, but unfortunately, she couldn't protect me from every hurtful statement or action. Although she secretly wished she could follow me around the playground to defend off every second grader who would say a hurtful comment, it wasn't possible to deflect every harmful word.

In the midst of being unable to protect her children from hurtful comments and actions, it is easy for *any* mom to feel guilt for the struggles her children face. Mothers of children with clefts may also experience additional guilt, contemplating whether they could have prevented the birth defect. Feeling like it's her fault, the mother may wonder if she took enough prenatal vitamins or if she accidently exposed herself to any harmful environmental chemicals while pregnant. She suddenly questions the places she lived, the foods she ate, and every action in between. While the Bible reminds us to not worry about our *tomorrows*, it's easy for some mothers to worry about *yesterdays*. Maybe it's not a constant guilt the mother feels; but in the mess of human emotions, at random times, the lie of "It's my fault" rears its ugly head.

Oh, the load moms carry. Mothers are so good at feeling guilt, in fact, they can even feel guilt for feeling guilty! But, of course, these emotions arise because these are mama bears who want to protect their cubs. A sense of duty and of deep responsibility for protection is ingrained deep within their fibers. Isn't this the very reason we love our mothers? They fight for us, protect us, and nurture us. Yet, what happens when life's circumstances, which the mother has no control over, brings harm to her child? What happens when her child has to endure multiple surgeries and all the mother can do is attempt to provide comfort after the surgery is complete? Even when the cause is completely out of the mother's control, she sometimes carries a sense of guilt that she should have done something better or differently.

When watching children go through struggles, guilt may heap upon us like falling rocks. Slowly, with each struggle, the rocks fall one by one. Some are like small pebbles, mere bumps in the road. Others are huge and intensely burdensome, like boulders crashing upon us. It's in these moments, as each rock falls, when even the best mother may question, "Could I have done anything to prevent this for my child? Are their struggles *my fault?*"

Whose Fault is This?

I cannot speak firsthand to motherhood guilt. I'm not a mother; and I haven't felt the weight of it. However, scripture has changed my perspective on my cleft lip and palate in many ways. Interestingly enough, one passage also raises the question of whose fault is it when a child is born with a birth defect.

In John 9, we find the story of a man who was blind since birth. As Jesus and His disciples approached the man, his disciples asked,

"Rabbi, why was this man born blind? Was it because of his own sins or his parents' sins?" (John 9:2).

These words struck me. Why does it have to be someone's fault? Why is there always someone to blame? Is it possible that his blindness served a greater purpose?

"It was *not* because of his sins or his parents' sins'," Jesus answered (John 9:3).

Jesus responds concisely and clearly. This is NOT a result of *anyone's* sins.

Whoa.

It's not *my* fault.

It's not *my parents'* fault.

It's not *anyone's* fault.

Anyone raised in a law-based home or church, where punishment was prevalent and grace hardly extended, realizes the freedom of this statement. Through Jesus' declaration, we could hear; "God isn't mad at you" and "You didn't cause this to happen."

Jesus' statement lifts the burden of guilt and shame off of every mother who incorrectly has believed that she was to blame for her child's birth defect. It wasn't a rebellious past, it wasn't because you didn't attend church enough, and it wasn't because you didn't pray all the right prayers.

So, if no one is to blame, why was the man born blind?

Jesus answered, "*This happened so the power of God could be seen in him*" (John 9:3).

Revealing His power and glory, Jesus performs a miracle within this man. After spreading mud over the man's eyes, Jesus tells him to wash off in the pool of Siloam. After washing his eyes, the blind man could physically see![1]

When asked who healed him, the former blind man replied, "The man they call *Jesus*...."[2] The Pharisees called Jesus a sinner for healing on the Sabbath, but the man replied "I don't know whether he's a sinner, but I know this: I was blind, and now I can see!"[3]

Oh, I love that!

I *was* blind, but *now* I see!

I *was* lost, but *now* I'm found!

After performing the miracle, Jesus asked the former blind man: "Do you believe in the Son of Man?"

The man answered, "Who is he, sir? I want to believe in him."

"You have seen him," Jesus said, "and he is speaking to you!"

The man replied, "Yes, Lord, I believe!" and then started worshiping Him.[4]

The Pharisees and the former blind man were on a level playing field; they could all physically see Jesus standing before them. The Pharisees had complete vision since birth, yet they didn't have the spiritual eyes to recognize Jesus was the Son of God, the One who had come to set the captives free.

The blind man not only received his physical sight, but his spiritual eyes were opened as well. He now recognized Jesus as Messiah, the King of kings! What a shame it would have been, had the man gained his physical vision but hadn't gained the spiritual vision to recognize his need for a Savior.

I cannot help but leave this story, thinking about how the man's physical birth defect was what God *chose to use to bring glory to His Name*. Without the birth defect, there would have been no healing; and without the healing, we wouldn't have greater insight as to what it means to have our spiritual eyes opened to see Christ Jesus as Savior.

Seeing Jesus

As I finished reading this story in John 9, I realized that God revealed His glory through a miraculous physical healing. Even greater, He was glorified through a changed heart and eyes that see Jesus for who He is. Like the blind man, more than anything else, I want to see Jesus.

Do you know what is far worse than being born with a craniofacial anomaly? *Having eyes that cannot see Jesus.* Do you know what is worse than going through many surgeries? *Being blind to the person of Jesus Christ.* Do you know what is worse than receiving hurtful comments about your appearance? *Going through the heartache of this world without Jesus.*

With eyes to see Jesus, I realize I'm not the only one with scars. *Jesus Christ has scars as well.*

Although my scars are a result of a cleft lip and palate, Jesus Christ's scars remain from the nails driven into His hands and feet as He hung on the cross for *my* sins. God demonstrated the greatest love by sending His one and only Son to die on the cross so that we might have eternal life through Jesus.[5] Not waiting for us to love Him first, but while we were still sinners and away from God, He sent his Son as a sacrifice to take away our sins.[6]

Jesus is my Savior. I trust Him with my eternity. I trust Him with the scars on my lip. For too long, I have focused too much on the scars. Instead of focusing on my scars, I want to focus on Christ's scars. By seeing Jesus and making His scars the focus, I can now see this life clearly. By setting my eyes on the hope of Jesus Christ and eternity with Him, I can look past this temporary body and my frail attempts to find my value and worth in this world.

I am learning to see what really matters; and the things I once deemed important seem so trivial. I don't need more self-esteem or to think more highly of myself. I don't need to be more popular. I don't need the approval of others. I certainly don't need flawless physical perfection. While my desire for marriage isn't a bad thing, I don't even need to be married. I don't need to know every detail that will unfold in my life. I don't need to know how everything will turn out. I just *need* Jesus Christ.

When I first started wearing make-up, I had one desire: to find an amazing concealer that would hide my scars. I thought if I could cover my scars, no one would know I had a cleft lip and palate. I searched and searched, and none of them hid the scars as I had hoped. Today, with time and healing, hiding the scars on my lip is no longer the focus. Asking God to use my scars for His purpose is my primary concern. I no longer want to hide my struggles with having a cleft lip and palate. My main concern is sharing the hope I've found throughout my journey. Learning to take my eyes off myself, I'm learning to live for Him.

After all, today and for all eternity, *He is all that matters.* The grass will wither and flowers will fade. Jesus Christ will stand forever.[7] Although having a cleft has been a struggle at times, I want to focus on what matters for eternity, for only that which is done for Christ will last.

The Rearview Mirror

It's always sad when a vacation ends. As the packing up of belongings commences, there is a sobering moment of realizing that the precious moments we lived will soon be memories to cherish. Driving home from a relaxing vacation, I often gaze into the rearview mirror, soaking up one more visual memory of the beautiful scenery we enjoyed. Rearview mirrors. I love the glimpse they offer. In addition to serving as necessary driving protection, they also help us *briefly* look behind us. They help us to enjoy the fleeting moments we leave behind for just a second longer. While I refuse to live in the rearview mirror of my life, before I close this book, it seems appropriate to gaze back. With age and maturity, I take a quick look in my rearview mirror of life, now seeing with *open eyes.*

Looking back, I now understand my mother's compassionate heart. In the moment, I didn't realize that when I hurt, she hurt. When I struggled, she struggled. Her compassion extended to all of my siblings as well. If any of her children were disappointed, she felt and wore their disappointment. I want my mom to know that when I look back on the concern that she had for her children, I appreciate her tender love.

Not only was there emotional struggle, but there was physical pain as well. When I was going through the surgeries, I experienced some pain. Although I never looked forward to the misery and discomfort that followed the surgery, I didn't realize that it was also a concern for my parents. One of the biggest struggles my parents had to endure was to watch their little kids endure pain. As an adult, my parents shared with me this struggle and stated they would have gladly taken my place if they could. Although they knew the surgery was best for me, they would have borne every ounce of discomfort if they could have taken my place.

I now see the everyday faithfulness and sacrifices that were made. My parents sacrificed parts of themselves, spending long hours and days going to and from doctor appointments. Finances were rearranged. They went without things so that I could get the care that was required. I see that clearly in my rearview mirror. While they believed they were just doing what any parent would do, I felt their love. I knew they cared. And I know they would do it all again if they were faced with the choice.

Looking just a bit longer into the rearview mirror, here is what I see. The cleft lip and palate is not my mom's fault. God formed my mouth, not her.[8] I see a young mother, doing whatever needed done, even if it meant sitting long hours, engaging in the slow and laborious process of feeding a baby with eating difficulties. I see a mom, forgoing her own supper, holding a baby in one hand and steadying the bottle with her chin as she occasionally grabbed handfuls of Cheerios to snack on, as she hadn't eaten all day.

I don't see a woman who let me down. I see a mother who

didn't have all the answers but did the very best as she knew how. She put one foot in front of the other into an unknown journey. She found her journey to be rocky at times. She was left battered and confused sometimes, but she always kept going. She had unanswered questions; and actually, she still has unanswered questions, but she never gave up on God.

I see a young mom who was learning to completely entrust her children to God. She was learning what it meant to trust Him in all things. I see a woman who remained strong in front of me when dealing with the struggles of the day, yet falling to her knees behind closed doors to shed her tears. I see a strong woman. She wasn't weak because she shed tears. She cried her tears well.

She taught me with her tears.

I see why the tears flowed. Tears flowed because she didn't like seeing her children suffer and was concerned for their future. She was never embarrassed of us. Tears flowed from concern of the rough road that was ahead. Tears flowed because she wasn't really sure if she was cut out for this job. I see a woman who felt very incapable while holding her infant with a cleft lip and palate; but time would prove that she was more than capable. God had given her everything she needed for the task ahead. With Christ in her, every mother of a child with a cleft lip and palate will prove more than capable as well.

Not only do I see a wonderful mom, but I see a *mighty* God. I see a little girl who was scared and fearful of the unknown, yet His strong and mighty hand *held me* secure. I see a *faithful* God who taught me to hear the truth of His Word instead of the names I had been called. I see a little girl who wouldn't speak, but a *life-giving* God taught her that words were not to be feared but rather a wonderful gift to share. And just for icing on the cake, He transformed a quiet and shy little girl into a Speech-Language Pathologist who now helps other children to learn to speak.

I see a *trustworthy* God, who didn't always remove the storm around me, but calmed the storm within me. I see the God of *comfort and compassion*, who comforted me in my struggles so that

I may comfort others. I see a *relational* God, who removed my false identities and labels, so He could become my all in all. I see a *perfect* God, who didn't make a mistake with how He formed me in my mother's womb. I see a *personal* God, who has a purpose for my life and ordained all of my days, before one of them came to be. I see an *intentional* God who brought amazing people into my life, who have encouraged my heart and helped me see from a different perspective than the lies I had believed. I see a *strong* God, who in my weakness, became my *strength.*

I pray you would know this God as well.

I See a Greater Purpose

The more I study the Word of God, the more I don't believe in mere random chance. Here we are. In our current situation. For this time. For a greater purpose than we realize. I'm now grateful that my parents couldn't "fix" it all or perfectly protect me from every heartache. Honestly, it wouldn't have been in my best interest.

As for the hurtful names that my parents feared I would be called, they, too, served a greater purpose. When you receive hurtful words, you learn to find refuge in the God who heals our wounds. In the times when I felt like my cleft made me ugly or not good enough, God worked those moments for my benefit. He taught me invaluable lessons...and has helped me share those lessons with you.

When the world tells you that you're not good enough, you look to the One who is good enough. When you're deemed not pretty enough, you run to the One who knit you together in your mother's womb. When you feel like no one else understands, you run to the One who understands. When you feel unchosen, the truth that God has chosen you and is calling you to His side is like water for a parched soul.[9]

If the inability to be deemed a beauty queen by the world's standards leaves me feeling empty and dissatisfied and this emptiness drives me to hunger for more of Christ, then I welcome the cleft lip and palate. If this physical imperfection opens my eyes to the vanity and unsatisfying nature of this world and leaves my soul hungering for eternal life with Christ, then I welcome my cleft lip and palate. If I have a cleft for ninety years while on this earth, and in my weakness and internal struggle, it draws me humbly to the foot of the cross, then I praise God for that. After all, in the end, the cross and my relationship with Jesus Christ is all that will matter for eternity.

I can confidently say that God has worked it for my good, as having a cleft lip and palate has taught me to see Jesus above anything in this world. Since experiencing the goodness of God through a personal struggle, I now know that *God will use it all*. With this perspective, we don't need to be hyper-focused on what happens to us in this lifetime. Rather, we can focus on allowing God to use all of it for His glory. Rather than being afraid of what may come, I want to spend all my days with my eyes toward heaven and hands extended, asking God to use it all.

All of me.

All of my joys and triumphs.

All of my struggles and disappointments.

Use it all.

And at the end of each day, no matter what life brings, I want to find myself in the arms of Jesus, the only place where I'm fully satisfied.

EPILOGUE: LOOKING AHEAD

After taking a final glance into the rearview mirror, I set my eyes upon the road ahead. I want to travel the remainder of my journey well. As an individual born with a cleft lip and palate, *I want to move forward.* I want to grow in truth, not circle around lies and struggles of the past. I don't want to spend my life figuring out who is to blame for every adverse situation in my life. I want to live my personal life unhitched from the lies that once bound me and stop falsely believing that I'm in control of each of my circumstances.

If I could offer one thing to mothers' hearts and minds, especially my own mom, I want them to rest in knowing that *it's not their fault.* I pray that if you're beating yourself up over things that you thought you could have done differently, that you would find rest in knowing that our God is in control. I don't want to rehearse the "What ifs?" in my own life; and I don't want you to rehearse them in yours.

I refuse to be caught up in "Why, God?"

Rather, I want to ask, "God, what do you want to do with this?"

"God, how can I glorify you *through* this?"

God is glorified when we see every hurdle as an opportunity to draw nearer to Him. God's glorified when we realize we aren't standing on shifting sand; we're standing on the Rock and need not fear. God's glorified when we praise Him and choose to dance in the rainstorms of life. God's glorified when an unbeliever looks at our lives and sees the transformation of mind and heart that only God could give, *even if our situation never changed.*

God's glorified when we praise Him even in our confusion and doubts. I want to bring glory to God, in the easy and the hard. I want to glorify Him when I understand His ways and when I have no clue what He is doing. I want to trust Him. I want to trust when my path is lit bright. I want to trust when I'm surrounded by darkness. Whatever I do, I want to do it for the glory of God.[1]

When we walk through challenging situations, we can praise Him for walking us through. We ask Him to take whatever Satan meant for harm and transform it for our eternal good. We ask Him to squeeze every ounce of good out of a bad situation. And then—we must open our eyes and ears to see and hear the good He is doing.

I want to see every hardship as an opportunity to lean into Christ and build my faith in the only One who can see me through. I want Him to use my experience with a cleft lip and palate to encourage others who walk a similar road. I want to be less concerned about my physical appearance and more concerned about the condition of my heart and my response to Jesus. I want to allow God to use everything in my life, even that which I would've never chosen for myself, to bring much glory to His Name. I want to lay it all down at His feet, surrendering it all, entrusting it to the One who is trustworthy in all things. And I want you to do it with me.

HIS SCARS: A PRAYER

Father,

May I *never* focus more on my scars than yours. The scars on your hands remain from the driven nails as you hung on the cross. And for my sins, demonstrating your great love, you sent Christ Jesus to die in my place.[1] Accepting you as my Lord and Savior, in undeserved kindness, you declared me righteous.[2] Nothing I have earned; and yet you paid my debt of sin and granted me eternal life through Jesus Christ.[3]

I pray that each person reading this book would see their need for a Savior and put their faith in you, accepting you as their Lord and Savior. You truly are the only answer for this dying and hurting world. I pray for the indwelling Spirit to do His work in our lives, empowering us to serve and glorify Christ Jesus.

> If you confess with your mouth that Jesus is Lord and believe in your heart that God raised him from the dead, you will be saved. For it is by believing in your heart that you are made right with God, and it is by confessing with your mouth that you are saved.....For everyone who calls upon the name of the Lord will be saved. (Romans 10:9-10; 13)

PRAYER OF SALVATION

If you have been encouraged by my testimony of the saving grace of Jesus Christ, I invite you to accept Him as your Lord and Savior as well. If you do, you can read aloud this *Prayer of Salvation* with me:

Dear God,

I am a sinner who is in desperate need of a Savior. I know I cannot earn eternal life on my own. I believe Jesus Christ is Your Son and through Him alone is the way to eternal life. In His kindness and love, He saved me by dying on the cross for my sins. Defeating hell, death, and the grave, He rose again victorious.

In His great mercy, He washed away my sins, giving me new birth and new life in Him. Now repenting from my sins, I ask Jesus to be the Lord of my life. Thank you for filling me with Your Holy Spirit so that I may live boldly for you.[1]

If you made a commitment to follow Jesus, I would love to hear about it!

Please contact me at deeperthanthescars@gmail.com to connect and share your story.

SCARS – I AM THEY

Songwriters: Matthew Armstrong, Mathew
Hein, Ethan Hulse, Jon McConnell
© Wordspring Music LLC

Waking up to a new sunrise
Looking back from the other side
I can see now with open eyes

Darkest waters and deepest pain
I wouldn't trade it for anything
'Cause my brokenness brought me to you
And these wounds are a story you'll use

So I'm thankful for the scars
'Cause without them I wouldn't know your heart
And I know they'll always tell of who you are
So forever I am thankful for the scars

I can see, I can see
How you delivered me
In your hands, in your feet
I found my victory

I'm thankful for your scars
'Cause without them I wouldn't know your heart
And with my life, I'll tell of who you are
So forever I am thankful

I'm thankful for the scars
'Cause without them I wouldn't know your heart
And I know they'll always tell of who you are
So forever I am thankful for the scars
So forever I am thankful for the scars

ACKNOWLEDGEMENTS

COGS Youth Group: You challenge me to dig into the Word of God and "Do Hard Things for God." David and Amber Schumacher and Jeff and Lori Rieman. I'm grateful for the opportunity to have worked alongside you. Thank you!

Pastor John Heyward: Thank you for taking the time to correct my Bible references when needed. I appreciate you taking the time to answer my many questions!

Matt Brubaker: Thank you for reading my rough draft and teaching me how to "show" rather than "tell" a story. Who knew two cousins with matching striped Osh Kosh overalls would one day grow up and publish books!

Lisa Betz: Thank you for your friendship. Your passion for writing encouraged me to never give up during this tedious process!

Jennifer Jeremiah: Thank you so much for editing the manuscript. Your feedback and corrections were instrumental to the completion of this book. I couldn't have done it without you!

Alison Lawrence, Annie Smith and Cassidy Tirmenstein: Your friendships were a true treasure during one of the most challenging yet fruitful times of my life. Fire Up Chips!

Stephanie Baker: I still admire your courage to share your story. Thank you for encouraging me to share my story with the Intro to Communication Disorders class. It helped me far more than you know!

Sharon Hetrick- It was no coincidence that you drove our excursion bus for our road games. Even though I was hundreds of miles from home, your care and love reminded me of home. I'm beyond grateful that God brought you into my life. You love others so well!

Maggie Donaker and Jonelle Diefenthaler: From BGSU graduate students, to "fellow speechies" and now lifelong friends. I'm blessed.

Dustin Rieman and Jodi Young: Very simply, you inspire me.

Katie Schumacher: Whether we're eating Thai or Mexican food, riding bikes or kayaking, our conversations always encourage me. You're real and authentic in all you do. Let's keep growing in the Lord together!

Terri Shive-Glover: Thank you for encouraging me throughout this writing process. Your feedback was instrumental in the creation of this book. I have enjoyed our conversations and growing in the Lord with you!

Aubrie Stechschulte- Thank you for encouraging me to go on adventures. God truly used this time to teach me more about Him. Also, thank you for your in-depth review of the rough draft.

Kim Lughibil: It surely was not a mutual love for cats that brought our friendship together! You have modeled to and encouraged me to dig deep into the Word of God. I'm forever grateful. Our many conversations led to the development of this book. Thank you!

Stephanie Hull: Nearly twenty years of friendship. Are we really that old? A friendship that started on a soccer field and basketball court has deepened through the years with our mutual desire to grow in the Lord. Oh, and you make me laugh. A lot. I enjoy "doing life" with you.

Curt Verhoff: We were inseparable growing up. You are always there for me. Buying me my first GPS system when I traveled to New York by myself, you showed genuine care for my well-being. Thanks for being a great brother.

Amanda Verhoff: I am thankful you became a part of our family. From the first day we met you, you felt like family. Thank you for loving my brother and being a great mom to my niece and nephews.

Angie Keck: Growing up, we couldn't have been any more different. Today, I couldn't ask for a better sister. From mutual respect to knowing I can count on you for anything, you're a huge blessing!

Scot Keck: Thank you for loving my sister well. You're a great brother-in-law and dad to my niece and nephew!

Keith Verhoff: I am grateful we share our cleft experiences together. You have a huge heart and always care for the well-being of others. I am thankful God made you my big brother.

Raelynn Keck, Hunter Keck, Fiona Verhoff, Silas Verhoff and Arlo Verhoff: I'm grateful God made me your aunt. I hope you know how much I love you. More than anything, I want you to know how much Jesus loves you and to serve Him all the days of your life.

Mom and Dad: I love you! Your love for the Lord and each other is evident in all you do. Your love and care for your children is always evident. What else can I say? You both have been rock solid through this journey.

Jesus: You are my everything.

NOTES

Introduction

1   "Cleft Lip and Palate," March of Dimes, January 2017, https://www.marchofdimes.org/complications/cleft-lip-and-cleft-palate.aspx.

Chapter 1: Leaving the Past in the Past

1   Hebrews 4:12
2   Matthew 7:3-5
3   John 13:31-37
4   John 13:38
5   John 18:13-27
6   John 21:15-18
7   Matthew 18:21
8   *Holy Bible New Living Translation*: Study Note on Matthew 18:21-35 (Carol Stream, IL: Tyndale House Publishers, 2008), 1616.
9   Matthew 18:22
10 *Holy Bible New Living Translation*: Study Note on Matthew 18:21-35 (Carol Stream, IL: Tyndale House Publishers, 2008), 1616.
11 Matthew 18:23-35
12 Colossians 3:13
13 Lamentations 3:22-23

Chapter 2: Removing the Label

1   1 Samuel 15:10-11
2   1 Samuel 20:14-15
3   1 Samuel 20:23
4   1 Samuel 31 and 2 Samuel 5:3
5   2 Samuel 9:3 (NKJV)
6   2 Samuel 9:6
7   Kay Arthur, *Our Covenant God* (New York: WaterBrook Press, 1999), 209.
8   *Holy Bible New Living Translation*: Study Note on Luke 16:21 (Carol Stream, IL: Tyndale House Publishers, 2008), 1741.
9   2 Samuel 4:4
10 *Holy Bible New Living Translation*: Study Note on 2 Samuel 4:4 (Carol Stream, IL: Tyndale House Publishers, 2008), 525.
11 Ephesians 2:10
12 1 John 1:9
13 Romans 5:8
14 Deuteronomy 7:6
15 Psalm 139:14 (NIV)
16 1 John 3:1
17 1 John 4:4
18 James 2:23 and Colossians 1:27
19 Ephesians 2:10
20 2 Corinthians 5:20
21 Luke 15:11-31
22 "Lexicon: Strong's H2142 – Zakar," Bible Blue Letter, August 2019, https://www.blueletterbible.org/lang/lexicon/lexicon.cfm?Strongs=H2142&t=KJV.
23 Ephesians 1:3-8
24 Revelation 3:20
25 *Holy Bible New Living Translation*: Study Note on Revelation 3:20 (Carol Stream, IL: Tyndale House Publishers, 2008), 2172.
26 *Holy Bible New Living Translation*: Study Note on Luke 14:13 (Carol Stream, IL: Tyndale House Publishers, 2008), 1738.

Chapter 3: The Power of Words

1 Thomas G. Long, Testimony: Talking Ourselves into Being Christian (San Francisco: Jossey-Bass, 2004), 85-86.
2 Proverbs 12:18
3 Luke 6:45
4 Psalm 19:14
5 Psalm 141:3

Chapter 4: A False Identity Shattered

1 2 Corinthians 4:7
2 2 Corinthians 12:9-11
3 1 Peter 1:7-8
4 2 Corinthians 4:17-18

Chapter 5: Rejection

1 Micah 6:8
2 Nancy DeMoss Wolgemuth & Dannah Gresh, *Lies Young Women Believe and the Truth that Sets them Free* (Chicago: Moody Publishers, 2018), 87, 88.
3 Psalm 84:11
4 Luke 4:1-13, Matthew 10:25, Matthew 27:39-42, Matthew 9:23-25
5 Matthew 8:34
6 Luke 4:16-30
7 Isaiah 53:3
8 *Holy Bible New Living Translation*: Study Note on John 13:21 (Carol Stream, IL: Tyndale House Publishers, 2008), 1799.
9 Hebrews 4:15
10 Hebrews 2:17-18
11 Romans 8:34

Chapter 6: Finding True Strength

1   Hebrews 5:7
2   John 11:35
3   John 11:38
4   "Definition of Lament," Merriam Webster Dictionary, August 24, 2019, https://www.merriam-webster.com/dictionary/lament.
5   Matthew 27:46
6   Psalm 56:8
7   Psalm 34:18
8   Psalm 30:5
9   Matthew 11:28
10 Revelation 21:4
11 David T. Lamb, *God Behaving Badly* (Downers Grove: Intervarsity Press, 2011), 157.
12 David T. Lamb, *God Behaving Badly* (Downers Grove: Intervarsity Press, 2011), 156.
13 Ecclesiastes 3:4
14 Psalm 138:3
15 Psalm 40:5
16 Psalm 94:14

Chapter 7: Fearfully and Wonderfully Made

1   *Holy Bible New Living Translation*: Study Note on Jeremiah 1:5 (Carol Stream, IL: Tyndale House Publishers, 2008), 1208.
2   Esther 4:14
3   Matthew 10:30
4   John 10:3
5   Galatians 2:20
6   James 1:18
7   Revelation 4:11
8   Genesis 1:31
9   Vanessa Van Edwards, "Body Types Through History," accessed March 10 2020, http://www.scienceofpeople.com/ideal-body-types-throughout -history/.
10 Psalm 139:14

Chapter 8: Victory in Death and the Hope of Eternal Bodies

1   Hebrews 2:14-15
2   Revelation 1:18
3   2 Corinthians 5:8
4   Philippians 1:21 (NIV)
5   Philippians 1:23, John 5:24, John 11:25-26
6   Romans 8:18-22
7   2 Corinthians 5:1-2
8   2 Corinthians 5:4-5
9   1 Corinthians 15:51-53
10   Dr. David Jeremiah, "Revealing the Mysteries of Heaven: The Ultimate 'Extreme Makeover.'" 2017, DVD.
11   1 Corinthians 15:36-44
12   *Holy Bible New Living Translation*: Study Note on 1 Corinthians 15:37-39 (Carol Stream, IL: Tyndale House Publishers, 2008), 1951.
13   Romans 6:4-5
14   Luke 24:39
15   Matthew 8:11
16   1 Corinthians 9:24-25
17   Romans 8:23-25
18   2 Corinthians 5:1
19   1 Corinthians 15:42-49
20   Romans 6:13
21   1 Corinthians 6:19-20
22   Romans 14:7-9 and 2 Corinthians 5:14-15
23   Colossians 1:16
24   Romans 12:1

Chapter 9: Living as an Anomaly

1   Revelation 5:9
2   John 3:16
3   2 Corinthians 4:16
4   2 Corinthians 4:18
5   1 Peter 3:3-4
6   1 Samuel 16:7
7   Ephesians 5:1

8   Ezekiel 37
9   Ezekiel 36:26
10   Galatians 2:20
11   John 15:5
12   Isaiah 64:6
13   John 15:2-3
14   "Overview of Craniofacial Anomalies," Health Encyclopedia- University of Rochester Medical Center, accessed March 9, 2020, http://www.urmc. rochester.edu/encyclopedia/context.aspx?contenttypeid=90&content id=P01830.
15   Ruth 1:14
16   *Holy Bible New Living Translation*: Study Note on Ruth 1:14 (Carol Stream, IL: Tyndale House Publishers, 2008), 458.
17   Ruth 1:16
18   Ruth 2:7-12
19   Ruth 3:11

Chapter 10: Working All Things for Good

1   Romans 8:28
2   Dictionary.com, s.v. "Compassion," accessed March 9, 2020, https:// www.dictionary.com/browse/compassion.
3   "What is Compassion," UC Berkeley's GGSC, accessed March 9, 2020 http://greatergood.berkeley.edu/topic/compassion/definition.
4   Matthew 14:13-14
5   Luke 15:11-32
6   Psalm 34:19
7   2 Corinthians 1:6
8   Ruth 1:13, 20

Chapter 11: Cultivating Joy

1   1 Kings 19:4
2   Romans 15:13
3   Psalm 16:11
4   Hebrews 12:2
5   Psalm 95:1

6   Psalm 119:1-3
7   Galatians 5:22
8   Nehemiah 8:10
9   Philippians 4:4
10   Philippians 4:5-7

Chapter 12: Finding Malta

1   Philippians 4:19
2   1 Kings 18:36-37
3   1 Kings 18:34-35
4   1 Kings 18:38-39
5   Acts 28:1
6   Psalm 91:2
7   Matthew 11:28-29
8   Matthew 6:26-30
9   Matthew 6:33-34
10   Isaiah 26:3

Chapter 13: It's Not Your Fault

1   John 9:6-7
2   John 9:11
3   John 9:24-25
4   John 9:35-38
5   1 John 4:9
6   Romans 5:8
7   Isaiah 40:8
8   Exodus 4:11
9   Romans 8:30

Epilogue: Looking Ahead

1   1 Corinthians 10:31

His Scars

1   Romans 5:8
2   Romans 3:23-24
3   Romans 6:23

Prayer of Salvation

1   Titus 3:4-7

BIBLIOGRAPHY

Arthur, Kay. *Our Covenant God.* New York: WaterBrook Press, 1999.

"Cleft Lip and Palate." March of Dimes. January 2017. https://www. marchofdimes.org/complications/cleft-lip-and-cleft-palate.aspx.

"Definition of Lament." Merriam Webster Dictionary. August 24, 2019. https://www.merriam-webster.com/dictionary/lament.

DeMoss Wolgemuth, Nancy & Gresh, Dannah. *Lies Young Women Believe and the Truth that Sets them Free.* Chicago: Moody Publishers, 2018.

Dictionary.com. s.v. "Compassion." Accessed March 9, 2020. https:// www.dictionary.com/browse/compassion.

Jeremiah, Dr. David. "Revealing the Mysteries of Heaven: The Ultimate 'Extreme Makeover.'" 2017. DVD.

Lamb, David T. *God Behaving Badly.* Downers Grove: Intervarsity Press, 2011.

"Lexicon: Strong's H2142 – Zakar." Bible Blue Letter. August 2019. https://www.blueletterbible.org/lang/lexicon/lexicon. cfm?Strongs=H2142&t=KJV.

Long, Thomas G. *Testimony: Talking Ourselves into Being Christian.* San Francisco: Jossey-Bass, 2004.

"Overview of Craniofacial Anomalies." Health Encyclopedia-University of Rochester Medical Center. Accessed March 9, 2020. http://www.urmc.rochester.edu/encyclopedia/context.aspx?contenttypeid=90&contentid=p01830.

Van Edwards, Vanessa. "Body Types Through History." Accessed March 10, 2020. http://www.scienceofpeople.com/ideal-body-types-throughout -history/.

"What is Compassion." UC Berkeley's GGSC. Accessed March 9, 2020. http://greatergood.berkeley.edu/topic/compassion/definition.

CPSIA information can be obtained
at www.ICGtesting.com
Printed in the USA
BVHW070716100720
583333BV00002B/98